Contents

Acknowledgements

We would like to thank the Joseph Rowntree Foundation for their sponsorship of this research, especially Barbara Ballard, Principal Research Manager, and Shirley Dex, advisor to the Joseph Rowntree Foundation 'Work and Family Life' programme. Thanks are also due to the local authorities, 'Shopwell' and 'Cellbank', who generously agreed to participate. Our greatest debt is to the individuals within these organisations who agreed to be interviewed and who provided essential background information. Our thanks also go to our Advisory Group for their support: Vicky Daybell, Amanda Jones, Suzan Lewis, Diane Perrons, Niccola Swan, Mandy Wright and Clare Ungerson.

Introduction and background

In this research we address some of the consequences of the increase in married women's employment and thus a shift in the interrelationship between employment, work and family life. We will examine employment careers in three sectors: banking, retail and local government. Through an analysis of 126 work–life interviews with men and women, we will explore the extent to which family responsibilities are or have been compatible with individual career development. Have women who have taken a career break to raise children, or shifted to part-time working, been as successful, in career terms, as those who have not done so? How do employees manage their work, career and family responsibilities, and what is the impact of workplace pressures? Has the introduction of work–life integration policies had a significant impact, and what do employees think of these policies? Are men's and women's attitudes and behaviour very different as far as these issues are concerned? First of all, however, we will examine the recent historical developments that have given rise to these important contemporary questions.

The context

In 1911 women made up 29% of the labour force in Britain; by 1991 this percentage had risen to 43% (Crompton, 1997). This increase is largely a consequence of the growth of married women's employment. The level of women's economic activity grew steadily from the 1950s, and the pattern of married women's employment, particularly the employment of mothers, changed considerably over the last three decades of the 20th century. By the 1960s a 'bimodal' pattern of married women's employment had been established (Hakim, 1979). Most women left the labour force on the birth of their first child and returned to employment (often part-time work) when their youngest child started school.

Participation rates among women increased markedly during the 1980s, from 66% in 1984 to 71% in 1990. During the 1990s, rates were rather more stable, and reached 72% by 2001. In contrast, men's participation rates have been falling, from 88% in the 1980s to 84% by 2001. Participation rates for women have been rising fastest among mothers of young children. In 1990, the economic activity rate among mothers with a child under the age of five was 48% but by 2001 this had risen to 57% (Dench et al, 2002).

Thus "by the end of the 1980s it had become the norm for working women to be economically active again within nine months of having a baby" (McRae, 1996, p viii). These changes in levels of economic activity among women have run in parallel with both a rise in their levels of education and qualification, and policy developments that reflected women's increased economic activity and transformed aspirations. Since the 1979 Employment Protection Act, entitlements to maternity leave (and rights) have been gradually improved. 'Work–life balance' and 'family-friendly' employment policies are, increasingly, assuming a higher profile among policy makers (Forth et al, 1997; DTI, 2000; DTI/ HM Treasury, 2003). For even though women are, on average, now having fewer children, other caring responsibilities are growing. Changes in the delivery of health and social care mean that this is increasingly being carried out within the household. Also, the population is ageing, so caring responsibilities for older people are becoming greater.

In parallel with changes in women's employment and family life, there has also been change and fluctuation in the economy, in organisations and in the labour market. In the 'older' industrial countries such as Britain, manufacturing and the older extractive industries are in decline and there has been a shift to service employment. The experience of economic recession in the 1980s was accompanied by the rapid expansion and development of new managerial techniques. Increasingly, competition between enterprises was focused on the nature of service provision (and thus employee performance) as companies strove to develop cultures of 'excellence' (Peters and Waterman, 1982), and 'high commitment' management strategies were developed. Another complementary strand of the new managerialism developed a critique of existing (bureaucratic) organisational structures and emphasised the cost savings to be gained through downsizing, dismantling bureaucratic structures through 'delayering', and promoting the 'lean organisation' (Kanter, 1977; Womack et al, 1990).

Throughout this period, there has also been an increase in the extent of flexible employment, which can include shift work, part-time work, working at home, annualised hours, the use of agency workers and so on (Dex and McCulloch, 1997; Purcell et al, 1999). Up until the 1980s, the dependence of the full-time career man upon the services of a non-working 'career wife' was an established fact (Finch, 1983; Crompton, 1986). This particular employment/family arrangement corresponded to the 'male breadwinner' model, in which men specialised in market work while women specialised in unpaid caring and domestic work, and the male careerist was enabled to devote himself to full-time employment. Thus the majority of women did not have employment 'careers'. However, the more recent development of employment flexibility, together with shorter job hierarchies in 'delayered' organisations and increased sensitivity to the necessity for 'family-friendly' employment, might, in the abstract, provide more favourable circumstances for individuals wishing to combine an employment career with caring responsibilities.

However, recent empirical work suggests that caring responsibilities continue to present problems for people wishing to pursue organisational careers. In their comparative study (of banking, nursing and local government),

Halford et al (1997) suggest that in relation to careers, gender discrimination as such has been replaced by a distinction between 'encumbered' and 'unencumbered' employees: that is, those with and without caring responsibilities. In the US, Hochschild's (1997) work suggests that, even in an organisation that had a prominent 'family-friendly' profile, competitive pressures resulted in longer hours for working parents and the eventual collapse of family-friendly policies. Nevertheless, there have been important developments over the last decade, and suggested employer-related policy improvements include a range of provisions such as flexible working patterns, carers' leave and other help such as day care and specialist advice.

The study

Building on a previous project (Employers, Communities and Family-friendly Employment Policies, subsequently referred to as ECFFEP; see Yeandle et al, 2002) we have carried out in-depth interviews in two localities (Sheffield and East Kent/Canterbury) with 126 men and women. The sectors of employment investigated have been banking (Cellbank), retail (Shopwell) and local government. Thus we have carried out interviews in Shopwell stores and Cellbank retail branches in Sheffield and East Kent, as well as in Sheffield and Canterbury City Councils. None of the men interviewed had taken a voluntary employment break on account of family responsibilities, but one man had changed his hours of work for this reason. Of the 84 women interviewed, 41 had taken a complete employment break because of family responsibilities, 26 had changed their working hours, and 17 had neither taken a break in employment nor changed their working hours. In brief, our objectives were:

- to explore the impact of flexible working and employment breaks on individual careers for men and women in three contrasting employment sectors;
- to assess the impact of organisational culture on the take-up and impact of family-friendly policies: for example, are they artifacts (Lewis, 1997) that are contradicted by basic assumptions, such as long hours working, that work against them?
- to explore men's attitudes to family-friendly working arrangements.

The nature of the localities

The ECFFEP study revealed a number of differences between the two localities. Sheffield has a more static population and a higher level of unemployment than Canterbury/East Kent. The extent of alternative, local authority-funded care provision (for example, local authority nurseries, after-school clubs), is greater in Sheffield. Thus the caring facilities available to our interviewees were slightly different. For example, two of our Sheffield interviewees reported using local authority nurseries, not generally available in Canterbury. The ECFFEP project found that respondents in Sheffield were more likely to be able to draw on family help – particularly grandparental help in the case of children – than respondents in Canterbury, reflecting the lower level of geographic mobility that prevailed in Sheffield. Employed people with childcare responsibilities in Canterbury make greater use of formal care provision such as paid babysitters, day nurseries, after-school clubs and so on.

In both localities, therefore, employed carers make use of the same kinds of formal and informal care facilities, but the extent of the availability of these facilities varies between the localities. However, this research has a focus on individuals rather than aggregates. The individual-level accounts of employment and caring given by our interviewees do not bring these locality differences, real though they are, into particularly sharp focus. Thus these differences are not a major feature of this report.

The nature of the organisations and their workforces

All of the organisations had formal policies for (extra-statutory) maternity, paternity, adoption, parental and carers' leave, as well as for part-time working and job share. At the time of the ECFFEP survey (2000), most of the additional leave options were available only on an unpaid basis. Cellbank additionally offered some leave options on a paid basis, including carers' leave, emergency leave and compassionate leave. Sheffield City Council and Shopwell employees were both entitled to paid adoption and paternity leave, and both councils also offered paid compassionate leave, although this was discretionary.

From the ECFFEP survey, we can derive a summary description of the characteristics of the labour force in the three organisations. There were systematic differences in qualification level between the respondents in the three organisations. In the two local authorities, respondents' academic qualifications clustered at 'A' level and above. In Cellbank qualifications clustered around the GCSE/'O'/'A' level. In Shopwell, however, over 70% of employees had either only GCSEs or no qualifications. Employees in Sheffield were on average older, and had longer service with their organisations than employees in Canterbury/Kent (reflecting the relative lack of geographical mobility in Sheffield). Nevertheless, there were also marked differences between the three organisations that went in the same direction in both localities. Sixty-seven per cent of Shopwell employees had less than five years' service, as compared to 24% of council employees and only 16% of Cellbank employees. These differences will obviously have an effect on the extent to which the individuals interviewed have had the opportunity to build careers in the organisations studied.

Research methods

In this project, we have gathered further information relating to the kinds of promotion opportunities and career paths available within the case study organisations (see Chapter 2). We have also carried out interviews with individuals in each case study organisation who have either taken an employment break and/or moved to part-time working, as well as those who have not. Within each organisation, these 'flexible working' individuals have been matched with similar employees who have had a continuous employment career. The same structured interview schedule has been used in all interviews (Appendix A). Interviews have been transcribed, and analysed using NVivo (a computer-aided qualitative data analysis package).

As we have seen, the three organisations drew on rather different segments of the labour market, as reflected in the different levels of qualification among employees. Thus we have held – as far as possible – levels of education/qualification (as well as age and organisation) constant in carrying out the matches. There are also marked differences between the employment/family life cycles of women in different age groups. Every woman over the age of 45 whom we interviewed had taken an employment break if they had had children, but as we shall see, many of the younger women, to varying degrees, had remained attached to employment. The analytical requirement to hold education levels constant, together with the contrasting behaviour of different age cohorts, put restrictions on our opportunities for making matches. The matching analysis is described in Chapter 2, and in Chapters 3 and 4 we have carried out a thematic analysis of all interviews.

The selection of our interviewees was not random but purposive. In each organisation, we requested interviews with men and women with particular employment histories (including whether or not they had taken an employment break and/or moved to part-time working), and in particular age categories. We do not, therefore, claim to have interviewed a representative sample of employees. Given the nature of the project, it is also the case that most of those who came forward for interview had caring responsibilities, and in some cases these were quite heavy. Thus this report will be developing an in-depth, rather than strictly representative, analysis of individual attitudes to and strategies of employment, careers and caring in the three sectors.

Each interviewee has been given a pseudonym, and a full listing of interviewees, together with basic information, is given in Appendix B.

Flexible working and employment careers

Employment careers in contemporary organisations

A significant aspect of economic restructuring and the development of the new managerialism from the end of the 1970s was the supposed end of the bureaucratic career and the development of the 'portfolio career' (Handy, 1994). Individuals would no longer rely on structured progress through an organisational hierarchy in order to develop their careers, but would rather self-develop their own career paths as they moved from job to job, company to company[1]. The actual frequency of such 'portfolio career' development has proved to be rather less than anticipated (Wacjman and Martin, 2001). Nevertheless, it might be argued that the development of the 'boundaryless career' (Arthur and Rousseau, 1996) might facilitate the combination of both employment *and* caring 'careers', as the self-developed individual is less dependent on the organisation per se to provide him/her with opportunities for advancement. As Kanter (cited in McGovern et al, 1998, p 460) puts it: "reliance on organisations to give shape to a career is being replaced by reliance on self". In such a model, individuals might make their own strategic choices as to the integration of employment 'work' and caring 'work'. In principle, if individuals are becoming less reliant on 'organisational assets' – that is, service with, and knowledge of, a particular organisation (Savage et al, 1992) – in order to develop an employment career, then the career penalties associated with, for example, breaks in organisational employment, should be less severe than they were in the past.

Careers within contemporary organisations have been much affected by new managerialist developments, including restructuring and 'delayering'. A wide range of literature has documented growing managerial insecurity associated with a decline in middle management positions and an increasing emphasis on self-development (for a summary see McGovern et al, 1998). In some contrast to the positive scenario described above, one of the negative aspects of these developments, from the perspective of work–life integration, is of perceptions of career insecurity leading to the growth of a long hours culture as individuals seek to demonstrate their worth to the organisation.

Not surprisingly, much of the emphasis in recent discussions of the impact of organisational restructuring on individual career development has been on managerial occupations. However, Grimshaw et al (2001, 2002) have recently argued that another significant effect of recent changes in service sector organisations has been to open up the 'gap' in the job ladder between lower grade employees and the first step on the promotional ladder: "the most direct effect of the flattened jobs hierarchy has been to remove the architecture necessary for career progression" (Grimshaw et al, 2001, p 38). Grimshaw et al studied four large service sector organisations (community care provision, retail, telecommunications services and telebanking). In all of these organisations, the intermediate grades in the job hierarchy had disappeared. Employers and managers had introduced a number of strategies, including multiskilling and teambuilding, in order to offset the adverse impact of delayering on workers' expectations. However, these had not been particularly successful. Rather, making the transition to the first rung of the managerial ladder had become

---

[1] For a more negative assessment of the 'portfolio career', see Sennett (1998).

increasingly dependent on individual appraisals, and Grimshaw et al argue that "staff with ambitions to 'move up' the organisation ... know that they face an 'all-or-nothing' effort in time and energy to make the transition to a mid-level post. They also know that if they are successful they will be faced with an enormous increase in the responsibilities they face and associated pressures on their working time" (2002, p 109).

Women and careers

Women currently make up only a minority of senior managers. The absence of women from managerial positions, despite their increased level of participation in paid employment, has been widely debated. Early discussions of the topic tended to be preoccupied with equal opportunity issues, and had a focus on the obstacles faced by women per se in their attempts to gain entry into higher-level occupations and make progress through organisational hierarchies (for example, Kanter, 1977; Cockburn, 1991). During the 1990s, these discussions crystallised around the idea of a 'glass ceiling' (Davidson and Cooper, 1992) keeping women out of the topmost level of management. A parallel theme – and one that is emerging more strongly in recent debates – has been an emphasis on the significance of family responsibilities in shaping and limiting women's career progression. Evidence from empirical research in the 1970s and 1980s showed that women suffered occupational downgrading as they re-entered the labour force after a childrearing break (Dex, 1987). Recent studies of women in managerial positions have emphasised the difficulties they face in combining a managerial career with family responsibilities, and indeed there is evidence that these difficulties lead many women managers to limit their families or even forgo childbearing altogether (Halford et al, 1997; Wacjman, 1998; Crompton, 2001). Both organisational and family constraints remain significant, but in this study we will focus mainly on the impact of family caring responsibilities.

Although women's educational and employment levels continue to rise, housework and childcare seem to remain primarily 'women's work'. Thus as a recent comparative cross-national study of the careers of couples has concluded, there has been an asymmetric development of gender roles in recent decades. Although more wives/

partners have entered employment, husbands follow traditional career patterns and only in exceptional cases interrupt employment for family reasons (Blossfeld and Drobnic, 2001, p 379). The extent to which women disrupted their employment for family reasons varied between the countries studied by Blossfeld and Drobnic, but in all of the countries, the higher the education/qualification resources of individual women, the more likely they were to be in employment. Although, therefore, women in general are less likely to pursue careers than men, this general tendency is cross-cut by class factors, and women higher up the occupational order are more likely to remain in employment (and thus develop employment careers) than those in the lower reaches.

Careers in the organisations studied

In both Cellbank and Shopwell, recent changes had seen the erosion of organisational hierarchies and the 'delayering' of the organisational structure. For example, in Cellbank the number of grades was reduced from 14 to 7, and in Shopwell supervisor positions were downgraded. These changes have been accompanied by an emphasis on individualised career development in both organisations. Thus the organisational structure is relatively flat in both companies: only 6% of employees in the store were managers, and only 10% in Cellbank retail (where we carried out our interviews). Managerial grades in Cellbank begin at G4. In some contrast to Shopwell, Cellbank still retains a short promotion hierarchy (grades G1-G3) below the managerial grades.

The proportion of women managers is higher in other divisions of Shopwell, such as Head Office, where 28% of those on General Store Manager equivalent grades are women. In Cellbank as a whole, 67% of all employees are women. However, in Cellbank's Personal Financial Services (PFS), where we carried out our interviews, 80% of employees are women. The grade structure is biased towards the lower levels in PFS. For example, 42% of all PFS employees are G1, as compared to 24% in the group as a whole.

In the councils, the hierarchy of grades is less flat than in Cellbank and Shopwell, and in Canterbury City Council (CCC), for example, a third of all employees were grade 6 (G6) or above. In part, this will reflect the greater diversity of functions and services carried out and provided by the two councils. As we shall see, this diversity is reflected in a greater complexity of career paths in the councils.

Women were under-represented within the managerial grades of all of the organisations studied, although they were the majority of employees (figures include part-time employees). Of the total of female employees in each organisation, just over 3% of Shopwell (store), 7% of Cellbank (retail), and 17% of CCC were managers.

These figures can only give the most general indication of the structure of opportunities made available by the four employers we studied. In any case, our research objective is rather more specific: that is, to investigate the impact of flexible working and employment breaks on individual careers for men and women in the four organisations. We will do this via a close comparison of the careers of individuals who have taken employment breaks, or flexible employment options, with those who have not done so.

An individual may achieve employment breaks, and/or flexible working, either by changing a job – that is, leaving employment altogether or moving to a job with another employer, with more convenient working hours – or by taking advantage of the provisions (such as changed working hours) offered by the current employer. All of the organisations studied offered these kinds of 'family-friendly' policies to their employees. However, as we shall see, employees at Shopwell had on the whole achieved flexibility by moving between different employers (and self-employment), whereas employees in the councils and more particularly Cellbank, had used the opportunities for flexible working offered within their organisations.

Analysis of matched cases

As we have seen from our previous discussions, gender is *the* most important factor determining whether or not an individual takes an employment break, or changes their employment arrangements, on account of caring responsibilities (Blossfeld and Drobnic, 2001).

After gender, age is the next most important factor not least because, before 1973, there were no statutory entitlements to maternity leave in Britain, and in any case there were strong normative expectations that young children would be exclusively cared for by their mothers. After age, the next most important factor shaping the employment behaviour of women is level of education, in that mothers with higher levels of education are more likely to be in employment than those with lower levels of education.

These aggregate trends have affected the possibilities we had available in carrying out the matching exercise. None of the mothers we interviewed over the age of 45 had *not* taken an employment break. All of the female matches over the age of 45, therefore, are between women with and without children.

We have also seen that it has been argued that organisational assets per se are becoming less important in individual career development. However, this implies that, conversely, an *individual's* assets – particularly education and qualifications – are becoming more significant in career development. It is very important therefore in attempting to assess the significance of employment breaks on career development, that individuals with similar levels of qualification are matched with each other. We have followed this principle in generating the matches. As described in the previous chapter, the nature of the labour market segments drawn on by the four organisations were rather different, particularly in respect of education levels. Employees in the councils had the highest levels of qualification, employees in Shopwell the lowest, with Cellbank employees somewhere in between. These organisational differences in education levels, therefore, have restricted the possibilities of matches across organisations.

In total, we carried out 126 work–life history interviews with 84 women and 42 men (Appendix B)[2]. We made 20 matches between women and women, and 33 matches between men and women. Although these interviews were in no sense a random sample, the characteristics of our interviewees nevertheless reflected, in broad outline, the gendered national, occupational and class trends we have already discussed. Except for a single case, men

---

2   All interviewees have been given pseudonyms.

had not taken employment breaks or changed their working arrangements because of caring responsibilities, whereas the great majority of women with caring responsibilities had done so. The impact of women's educational and occupational level was also apparent in the workplaces studied. In both Cellbank and the councils (where the educational/occupational levels among women were higher), the younger women interviewed tended to remain attached to employment (often part-time employment) when their children were young, whereas younger women in Shopwell were more likely to take employment breaks.

Shopwell: caring and careers

Shopwell had the flattest grade profile of the organisations studied. Although in principle therefore careers in Shopwell were open to all, few will actually rise up the career ladder. Many of the men working in Shopwell had had working lives punctuated by redundancy and/or breaks in employment and had been relatively unsuccessful in employment career terms. In the case of Shopwell, therefore, employment careers had been shaped more by external class factors, and breaks in employment as such were not significant within the Shopwell organisational context as far as promotion was concerned.

At the shop-floor level, work at Shopwell was extremely flexible: indeed, for many interviewees this flexibility was an important reason for working there. However, managers tended to work long hours. A match between Alice and Gemma, both of whom left school with 'A' levels, describes the contrasting career fates of women with and without breaks in employment (Figure 1).

Alice's employment history includes a series of part-time jobs as well as occupational downgrading.

Alice: "I was working for [government department]. In the time I took maternity leave for my oldest it became combined with [another department]. So it was a whole new building, a whole new manager, it completely changed. When I came back everything had changed. Still managed a career for myself and still got the recognition, but the manager didn't like

part-time workers, didn't like mums. I took six months [maternity leave] for each of them. No, correction, I took a career break from the [department] but I still carried on working in another job. When my career break finished at the [Department] I left officially.... The reason I didn't go back [to employment] after my third was because I physically couldn't do it.... The reason I'm here is not the money, believe me. It's the flexibility that I get here that makes it worth staying for."

Gemma, in contrast, has had unbroken employment and has gained further qualifications. She also works 55 hours a week.

The chequered employment careers of mothers who juggle with childcare responsibilities is further illustrated by the match between Donna and Sean, both aged 30, and both with a child under the age of 10 (Figure 2).

Donna: "I lost my job when I was pregnant and so I took a part-time job when he was eight months old, then I took over the business [hairdresser]. It was a new business and I kept it going but I didn't have enough money to put into it so I decided to give it up.... Then I worked at a bakery on night shifts just for a wage. It didn't have any career prospects. I was a hairdresser before but had had enough of it and childcare was difficult to arrange in the day times. Now I only struggle when the school holidays come around.... It is one big juggle."

Donna wanted to make a career and at some point hoped to go to university, but as she said: "I could have taken further steps if I didn't have childcare but until now I've not really been able to get opportunities because of childcare". Sean, in contrast, has never had a break in employment.

The complex work–life experiences of women with relatively low levels of qualification may be further illustrated by the contrast between Grace and Elena (Figure 2). Elena worked as a hairdresser until her first child (when she was 20). When he was 18 months old she started to do evening work at a nearby factory. Her second child was born when she was 25. She took a year off from work then went back to the

Figure 1: Shopwell: Alice and Gemma

Alice: 35, shop floor, 'A' levels
Gemma: 38, manager, 'A' levels, professional qualification

Work	Alice	Family	Age	Family	Gemma	Work
Full-time study			15			Full-time study
			16			
			17			Full-time work
Full-time work			18			
			19			
			20			
		Married	21			
			22	Married		
			23			
Six months maternity leave, Part-time work		Child 1	24			
			25			
			26			
Six months maternity leave		Child 2	27			
			28			
Left job, part-time work		Child 3	29			
			30			
Six months maternity leave		Child 4	31			
			32			
			33	Divorced		
			34			
Shop floor			35	Married		
			36			
			37			
			38			Manager

Full-time study
Full-time work
Part-time work
Full-time at home

Figure 2: Shopwell: Donna and Sean

Donna: 30, shop floor, NVQ
Sean: 30, shop floor, City and Guilds

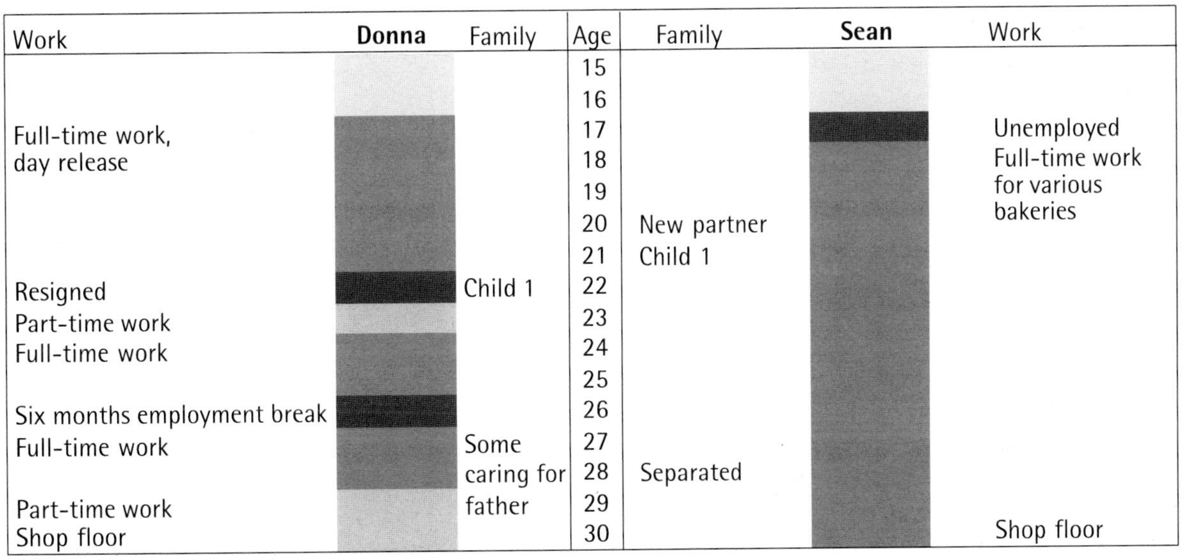

Work	Donna	Family	Age	Family	Sean	Work
			15			
			16			
Full-time work, day release			17			Unemployed
			18			Full-time work
			19			for various
			20	New partner		bakeries
			21	Child 1		
Resigned		Child 1	22			
Part-time work			23			
Full-time work			24			
			25			
Six months employment break			26			
Full-time work		Some	27			
		caring for	28	Separated		
Part-time work		father	29			
Shop floor			30			Shop floor

factory (evening work) until the age of 32. She then started working part time in a nursing home. Two years ago she started working at Shopwell part time. In contrast, Grace has never taken a break from employment, although she worked part time (in the school meals service) when her children were young. Grace has been working for Shopwell for four years, during which time she has been promoted to manager. Neither Elena nor Grace thought of themselves as a 'career' person.

> Elena: "You can always work up the ladder, as far as management. I wouldn't want to go that far. Too much responsibility."

> Grace: "I know it's contrary to what I'm doing, but I've always classed myself as a family person."

It is not possible to say how much Grace's career development (in contrast to Elena's) has been as a consequence of her lack of employment breaks. In her present job, however, she often works long hours: "[You work] 45 [hours] contracted, but can do 50, 55, 60 depending on how bad your department is. Because, as a manager, you are responsible for your department. So if there is a lot of sick, like there is at the moment, you won't get your two days off".

Shopwell has a wide range of family-friendly policies and, indeed, family-friendliness is an important aspect of the ethos of the company. These policies are much appreciated by Shopwell employees at the lower level. However, as we have seen, managers at Shopwell work very long hours, and this may be used as a measure of commitment to the company.

> Daniel: "I used to work longer hours to get promotion, you have to show you're committed by putting the hours in. They don't stress that but you do it yourself."

As one manager (Martin) answered when asked a direct question as to whether Shopwell was 'family friendly':

> "No, not at all. I know they are driving towards being family friendly. When I first walked into the store it was, 'You will work a minimum of 50 hours a week'. None of this we are downgrading [that is,

downshifting] or anything, you will work a minimum. You know straight away you are going to do more than 50 hours."

The flexibility Shopwell offers for shop-floor staff is accompanied by relatively low wages. Among the 32 Shopwell interviewees, 16 reported *household* incomes of less than £20,000 a year (12 had incomes of less than £15,000 a year). All of the seven managers interviewed reported household incomes of more than £30,000 a year but, as we have seen, they usually worked long hours and their jobs could hardly be described as 'family friendly'.

Cellbank: caring and careers

Of the three organisations studied, Cellbank had the longest-serving employees and therefore the largest proportion among those interviewed who had developed their careers within the organisation. Banking was once considered a 'job for life', and the location, par excellence, of the bureaucratic career. Young men were carefully guided through the banking hierarchy, and a comfortable salary, with employment security, might reasonably be expected by their mid-forties[3]. This situation has changed dramatically. Banking is no longer a 'job for life'[4], and individualised career development has been introduced. All jobs within the bank are advertised (on a weekly basis), and individuals equip themselves for these positions through a combination of relevant work experience and the

---

[3] Extract from interview with bank manager, 1980: "Every new entrant comes in on a four-month probationary period. After two months we do an interim report. Depending on their qualifications on entry, and how well they perform during their probationary period, it may be that we will decide to mark them potentially for accelerated promotion.... Assuming that they join at 18: they've taken their 'A' levels and they come in shortly before they get their results. They are going to be in grade 1 for say 12-15 months. They are probably going to stay in grade 2 then for another 18 months to two years.... They may be in for as little as nine or ten months in grade 2. I would think that three years through the grades is probably.... In the first year, regardless of whether it's accelerated training or not, they are not assessed and advised of their position. They are assessed, but it's just on our records at that stage".

[4] Indeed, some of our interviewees were actively considering or had taken redundancy packages. They have not been identified in order not to breach confidentiality.

Figure 3: Shopwell: Elena and Grace

Grace: 40, manager, CSEs
Elena: 41, shop floor, CSEs

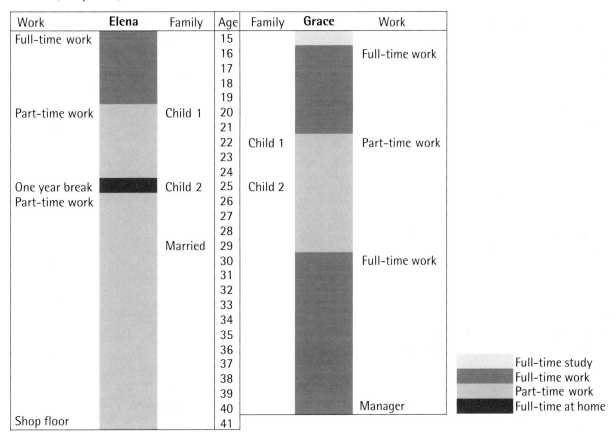

Work	**Elena**	Family	Age	Family	**Grace**	Work

Legend:
- Full-time study
- Full-time work
- Part-time work
- Full-time at home

completion of training packages/modules offered by the bank[5]. Nevertheless, because the great majority of Cellbank respondents *did* have long service, their employment profiles reflected their past career development within an 'old-style' bureaucratic organisation.

In the past, gender-discriminatory practices in banking led to a number of equal opportunities cases in the 1980s (Crompton, 1989). However, over the last two decades banks have developed into high-profile equal opportunity employers, and indeed the labour force in banking has become progressively more feminised. Banks were in the forefront in introducing career breaks and extended maternity leaves for women and, indeed, family-friendly policies have been further enhanced and developed in recent years. Thus, in Cellbank (and in some contrast to Shopwell), rather than move from job to job because of pregnancies and young children, women have

been able to change their working hours, at least for the last decade[6]. However, what has been the impact of this flexibility on career development?

In general, the Cellbank employees we interviewed who have taken career breaks or changed their working hours have not been as successful, in career terms, as those who have not done so although, as we shall see, there are exceptions to this rule. Our matches indicated that women who had not taken career breaks had done as well as men with similar levels of qualification, whereas those women who had taken breaks or changed their working hours had not. A 'stereotypical' example of the impact of employment breaks on women's career paths in banking may be found in the match of Tessa and Rupert, both of whom had joined the bank aged

---

5   It was once the case that professional banking examinations (ACIB, FCIB) were necessary for promotion. However, this no longer applies.

6   It may be noted that some women we interviewed had had to return to work full time after their first pregnancy, as part-time work in the bank had not been available to returners at that time. This situation, however, has now been improved.

Figure 4: Cellbank: Tessa and Rupert

Tessa: 49, grade 1, 'O' levels
Rupert: 46, grade 4+, ACIB

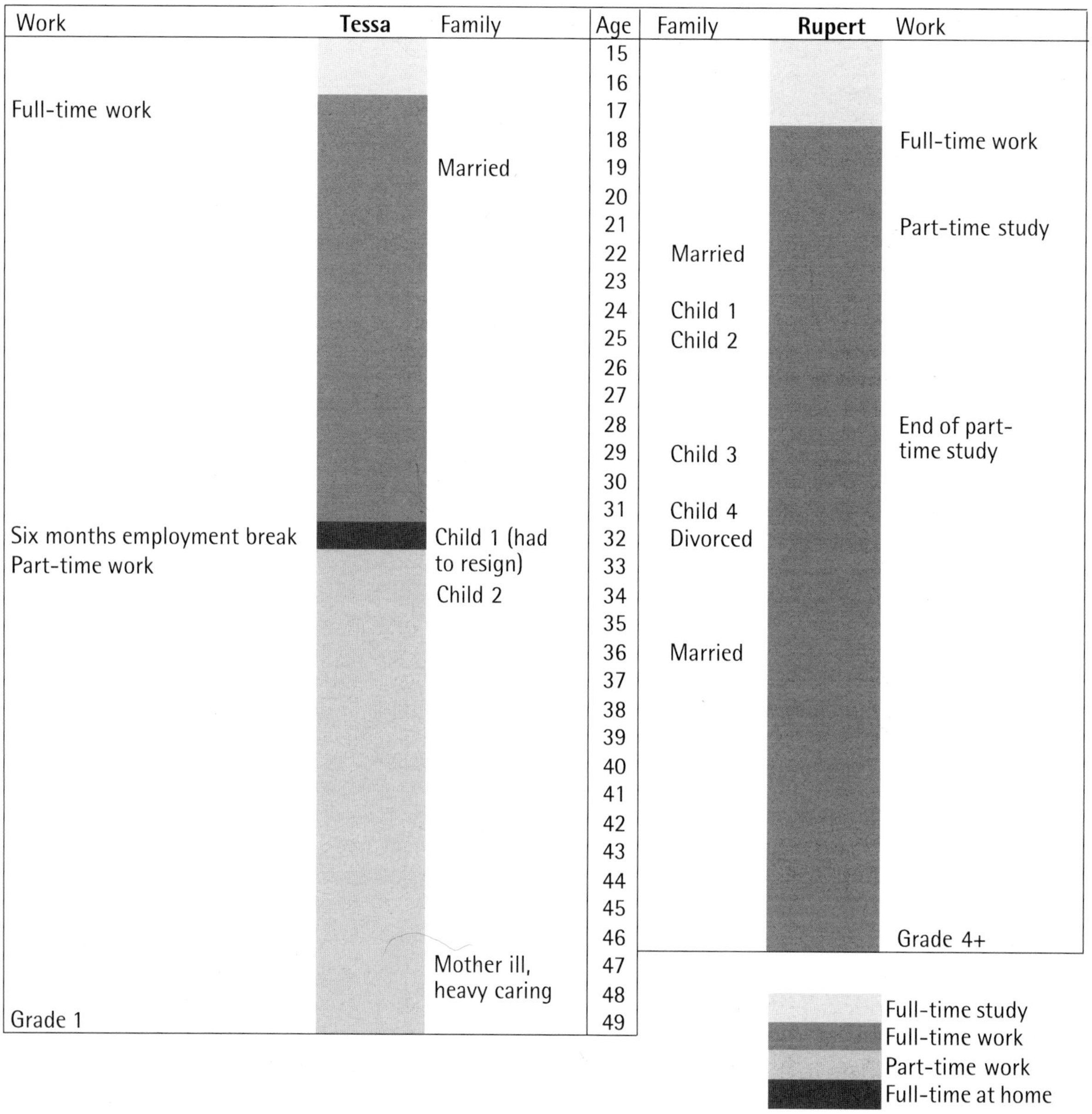

Work	Tessa	Family	Age	Family	Rupert	Work
			15			
			16			
Full-time work			17			
			18			Full-time work
		Married	19			
			20			
			21			Part-time study
			22	Married		
			23			
			24	Child 1		
			25	Child 2		
			26			
			27			
			28			End of part-time study
			29	Child 3		
			30			
			31	Child 4		
Six months employment break		Child 1 (had to resign)	32	Divorced		
Part-time work			33			
		Child 2	34			
			35			
			36	Married		
			37			
			38			
			39			
			40			
			41			
			42			
			43			
			44			
			45			
			46			Grade 4+
		Mother ill, heavy caring	47			
			48			
Grade 1			49			

Full-time study
Full-time work
Part-time work
Full-time at home

17, midway during their 'A' level courses. Both had found promotion slow (Figure 4).

Tessa: "In the first 15 years at the bank, it was quite difficult to progress quickly. When I left I was second cashier and it had taken me 10 years to get to that stage. I started at the bottom and worked my way through."

Rupert: "In the past it wasn't easy to get promotion; you needed the Institute of Bankers exam.... People didn't all take the exams and didn't always pass and sometimes it would take ages to pass

because you had to pass them all at one sitting."

Nevertheless, Rupert had gained his ACIB and is now grade 4+, whereas Tessa resigned from the bank at the birth of her first child (she was unable to return to her old job part-time so re-joined the bank, after resigning, as a 'peak-timer', which meant covering busy periods, such as lunchtime). Tessa has since increased her hours, but now has heavy caring responsibilities for her mother.

The impact of career breaks can also be seen in the contrast between Glenys and Shirley, both of

Figure 5: Cellbank: Shirley and Glenys

Shirley: 47, grade 3, 'O' levels
Glenys:48, grade 1, 'O' levels

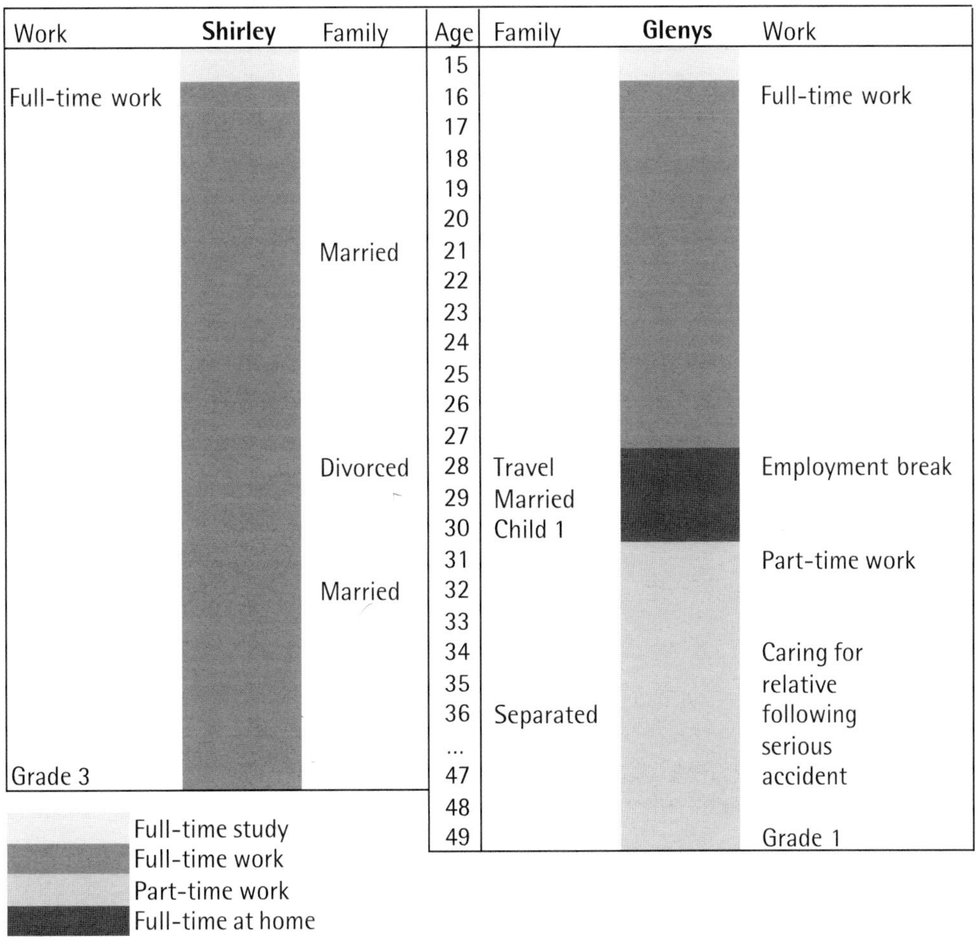

Work	Shirley	Family	Age	Family	Glenys	Work
Full-time work			15			Full-time work
			16			
			17			
			18			
			19			
			20			
		Married	21			
			22			
			23			
			24			
			25			
			26			
			27			
		Divorced	28	Travel		Employment break
			29	Married		
			30	Child 1		
			31			Part-time work
		Married	32			
			33			
			34			Caring for
			35			relative
			36	Separated		following
			...			serious
Grade 3			47			accident
			48			
			49			Grade 1

- ☐ Full-time study
- ☐ Full-time work
- ☐ Part-time work
- ☐ Full-time at home

whom joined the bank after their 'O' levels (Figure 5). Glenys had a career break, Shirley did not. Neither professes to be particularly ambitious, but Shirley is now grade 3 whereas Glenys (who also has caring responsibilities for a disabled relative) is grade 1. Thus an unbroken employment record is still of some significance as far as career progress is concerned.

Shirley: "I've had a gradual move up. I've been in the right place at the right time. If I was really ambitious I could have moved on quicker. This is as far as I could go in this side of the bank. I would have to move onto personal banker to move up but I don't want to. A lot of people have done so but I don't want to take all that on for what I'm paid."

Nevertheless, some women who had changed their hours or taken career breaks had advanced up the ladder, as the examples of Flora and

Peggy demonstrate (Figure 6). This match also provides a good example of the effect of changes in Cellbank policy over the years.

Peggy had resigned from the bank at the birth of her first child (because of the non-availability of part-time work), but from the age of 31 worked part time (including bar work as well as peak-time work in Cellbank).

Peggy: "I gradually built up my hours at the bank. I applied for a job as a personal banker but was told it was only full time. I was told to take it [she did, aged 35] and then apply for a job share but by the time a job share opportunity came up I was used to full time.... Women get more options now. They can have longer off work and it's a lot more relaxed. You can have quite a long break of up to one year. You can also pick your hours when you come back.... If I'd have had this sort of

Figure 6: Cellbank: Flora and Peggy

Flora: 41, grade 4+, 'A' levels
Peggy: 45, grade 4+, degree

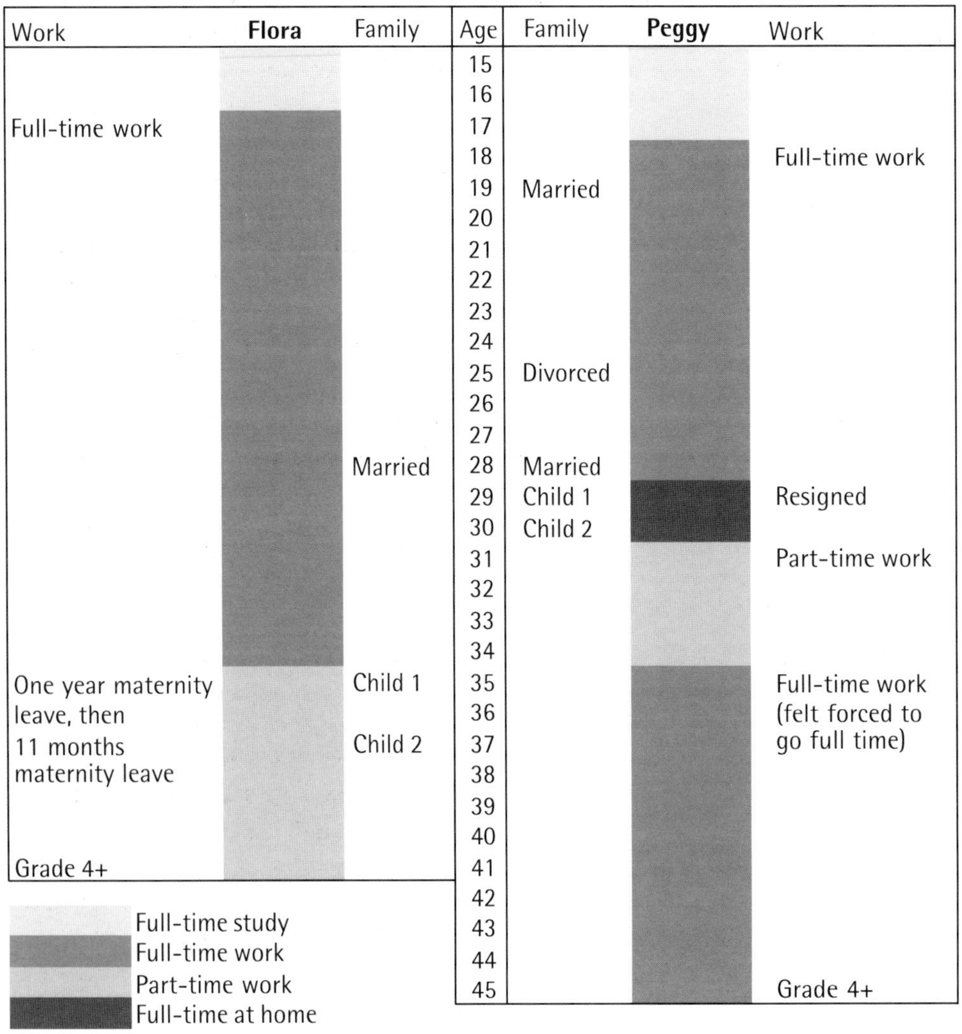

Work	Flora	Family	Age	Family	Peggy	Work
			15			
			16			
Full-time work			17			Full-time work
			18			
		Married	19			
			20			
			21			
			22			
			23			
			24			
		Divorced	25			
			26			
			27			
	Married	Married	28			
		Child 1	29			Resigned
		Child 2	30			
			31			Part-time work
			32			
			33			
			34			
One year maternity leave, then	Child 1		35			Full-time work (felt forced to go full time)
			36			
11 months maternity leave	Child 2		37			
			38			
			39			
			40			
Grade 4+			41			
			42			
			43			
			44			
			45			Grade 4+

Full-time study
Full-time work
Part-time work
Full-time at home

opportunity I would have gone straight back to work but there was no part time then, no flexibility."

Flora, who had had her children later than Peggy, had been able to take advantage of these new policies:

Flora: "After my first child I went on a career break, which was supposed to be a three-year part-time contract with the option of coming back full time at the end of that, but I fell pregnant again and then circumstances changed and you didn't need to go on a career break. The bank became a lot more flexible about juggling between full-time and part-time hours. But when I came back I was job-sharing: I did three days a week and my job share partner did the other two.... When I was pregnant with

my first child, I had actually started maternity leave and my job role disappeared. I went for a new job while I was on maternity leave and I was successful, but they had to put someone in for a year to cover my maternity leave, which was quite unusual, quite a big thing for the bank to do."

It is important to recognise, therefore, that the situation has shown considerable improvement over the years. Moreover, although Peggy had felt 'forced' to give up her job at the birth of her first child, because of the lack of part-time opportunities in 'career' jobs, she had nevertheless returned after a three-year break and had worked up to a promoted position (although not as quickly as Flora).

These improvements notwithstanding, there was widespread agreement that the higher people moved up the Cellbank hierarchy, the more difficult it became to combine employment with family life. The managers we interviewed all worked longer hours than contracted.

Flora: "I think the higher up in the bank you go, though, it just gets harder for the bank to be family friendly. They've still got the same policies there and I can still take advantage of the same policies that everyone else has, but it's harder for me to do that. It's a lot easier when you first join. [A senior person in the bank], even she, her husband has given up work to look after the children so that she can work full time, even she couldn't get the balance right. So there is a cut-off point where it becomes more difficult to be family friendly."

Peggy: "I keep getting told that I'd be selling myself short if I went part time. The bank does have flexible hours but the higher up you go you're not encouraged to take advantage of it."

Hannah: "I like my job and I want to work. I couldn't sit at home but I wouldn't let it affect my family life to be a manager. The higher up women go, they tend not to have kids."

Thus, as in Shopwell, in Cellbank managers work long hours and family-friendly policies are enjoyed largely by employees at the lower-grade levels.

The councils: caring and careers

Both Cellbank and Shopwell had career structures that applied to the organisation as a whole. There were relatively few divisions within these organisations and in both cases we interviewed in the retail divisions (that is, Shopwell stores and the Cellbank branch network).

In the councils, however, the situation was more complex. The diverse range of functions and services provided by the councils was accompanied by a parallel diversity of career paths. In many cases, local government careers would require the relevant professional qualifications: for example, in law, finance (CIPFA), librarianship, environmental health, and so on. As we have already noted, the level of educational qualification among council employees was the highest of the three sectors studied. Indeed, 12 of our 39 council interviewees were qualified at degree level or beyond (as compared to one Cellbank and one Shopwell interviewee, respectively). In general, therefore, it may be argued that the council interviewees were in a position to draw on more by way of 'individual' assets (or 'human capital') and were less dependent on 'organisational' assets than employees in Shopwell and Cellbank.

However, although the levels of qualification of the council employees might, in theory, render them more 'employable' on an individual level, many, nevertheless, had had careers in local government: indeed, more than 80% of Sheffield City Council (SCC) ECFFEP questionnaire respondents had over 10 years' service (as compared to 38% at CCC). At the higher managerial/professional level, it is often necessary to be geographically mobile in order to develop a career in local government, and this had been or was a problem for a number of interviewees (Green and Canny, 2003).

As in Cellbank, council employees who had not taken a career break and/or changed their working hours tended to have achieved higher-grade levels than people who had taken such a break. This tendency, however, was by no means universal and some women with heterogeneous employment careers had reached similar grade levels as had those without breaks.

An example of the impact of changed hours on career paths may be seen in the examples of Lorna and Anthony (Figure 7). Neither professed to be concerned with career maximisation: indeed, Anthony said he was not particularly interested in promotion as it would mean a longer journey to work in a different council office. Nevertheless, Anthony had progressed to a higher grade than Lorna.

Lorna, too, was not particularly interested in developing a career: "I see myself as having a career because of the length of time that I've been doing this job with the same employer but it's not that important to me". Nevertheless, she felt that working part time had had an impact: "I feel that some didn't like it because I came back

Figure 7: Council: Lorna and Anthony

Lorna: 36, grade 4-5, HNC
Anthony: 38, grade 6-9, 'A' levels

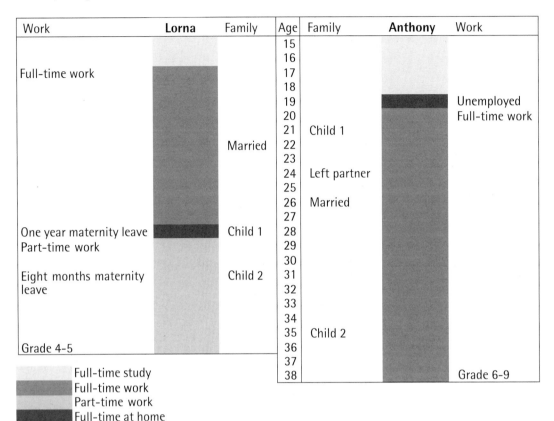

part time. I was seen as less important because I was working part time, so you miss out on things at work. I don't know if they mean to do it, or if they just forget because you're only around for half the week. I don't feel like I'm a true member of the team any more".

Women who had not taken a break or changed their hours had tended to move further in their careers than women who had done so, as can be seen in the comparison of Olga and Ursula, both of whom were qualified to degree level (Figure 8).

Olga was aware that she could develop a career if this had been her preference: "If I was career-minded ... the area that I work in has got a shortage, basically, so I'm always going to be able to get a job. If I was highly motivated I could get some really good jobs". Ursula, in contrast, had become more oriented towards a career with the passing of the years, in part stimulated by early opposition: "My boss at the time, he felt that it was the woman's job to stay at home until the children were five years old. He saw maternity leave as an inconvenience.... I

was determined to prove otherwise [that is, that women could combine family life and work]. I did the more difficult bits when I had two children. With my second I kept in touch with the office, and came into work half a day a week throughout maternity leave". It is obvious, therefore, that, motivational differences are very important in this comparative case, and the change in working hours per se is probably not the prime reason for the grade difference between the two women.

In both local authorities, there were examples of individual women who had been able to develop an employment career after a caring break. In the next example, Janine had not moved as far up the ladder as Alec, but had nevertheless been successful in building a career after a 10-year break (Figure 9).

The cases of Alec and Janine also serve to illustrate the complex employment histories of many of our council interviewees. In this there were some similarities with Shopwell employees, many of whom had had a variety of jobs (for example, Grace, Elena, Alice and Donna).

Figure 8: Council: Olga and Ursula

Olga: 41, senior officer, degree
Ursula: 44, senior officer higher level, degree

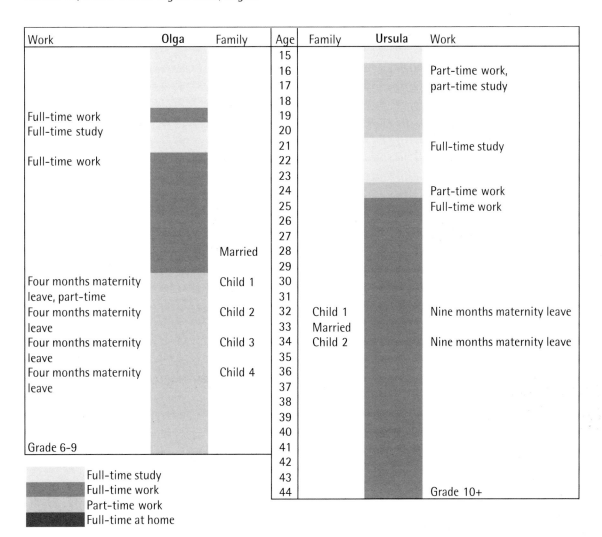

Work	Olga	Family	Age	Family	Ursula	Work
			15			
			16			Part-time work,
			17			part-time study
			18			
Full-time work			19			
Full-time study			20			
			21			Full-time study
Full-time work			22			
			23			
			24			Part-time work
			25			Full-time work
			26			
			27			
		Married	28			
			29			
Four months maternity		Child 1	30			
leave, part-time			31			
Four months maternity		Child 2	32	Child 1		Nine months maternity leave
leave			33	Married		
Four months maternity		Child 3	34	Child 2		Nine months maternity leave
leave			35			
Four months maternity		Child 4	36			
leave			37			
			38			
			39			
			40			
Grade 6-9			41			
			42			
			43			
			44			Grade 10+

Full-time study
Full-time work
Part-time work
Full-time at home

However, the generally higher level of education and qualification among our council interviewees meant that few had experienced occupational downgrading despite job changing and flexible working (for example, Janine had worked as an agency nurse during her career break).

In the two local authorities, there were also a number of cases of women in part-time employment at relatively senior levels: in addition to Olga, whom we have already discussed, there were also Rita, Nadine, Isobel and Eve. Here the councils may be contrasted with Cellbank, where as we have seen it was difficult (although not impossible) to work part time at senior levels. It may be noted that on the

whole in the councils these flexible senior women worked as specialists and/or professionals. As previous research has demonstrated, individuals with specific skills and competencies are able to work flexibly without loss of occupational status, but it is more difficult for those engaged in organisational careers in general management to do so (Crompton, 2001).

Both councils operated flexitime systems which were widely used (and appreciated). This meant that most employees in both councils did not work longer than their contracted hours, although in one CCC department interviewees complained that work pressures (following departmental reorganisation) made it difficult for

Figure 9: Council: Janine and Alec

Janine: 44, grade 4-5, 'A' levels
Alec: 43, grade 6-9, 'A' levels

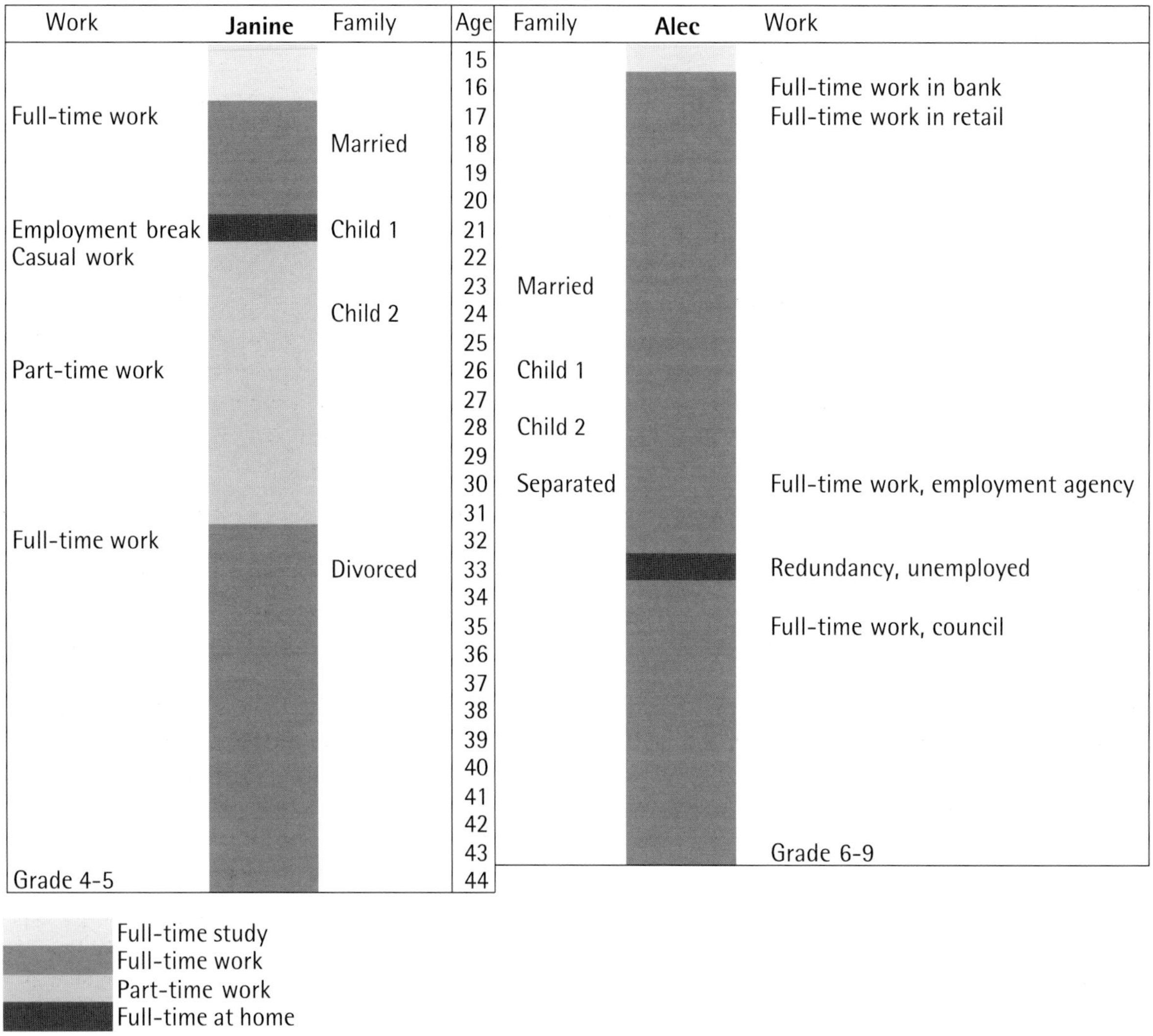

Work	Janine	Family	Age	Family	Alec	Work
			15			
			16			Full-time work in bank
Full-time work			17			Full-time work in retail
		Married	18			
			19			
			20			
Employment break		Child 1	21			
Casual work			22			
			23	Married		
		Child 2	24			
			25			
Part-time work			26	Child 1		
			27			
			28	Child 2		
			29			
			30	Separated		Full-time work, employment agency
			31			
Full-time work			32			
		Divorced	33			Redundancy, unemployed
			34			
			35			Full-time work, council
			36			
			37			
			38			
			39			
			40			
			41			
			42			
			43			Grade 6-9
Grade 4-5			44			

Full-time study
Full-time work
Part-time work
Full-time at home

them to take up their flexible entitlements[7]. In both councils, however, the more senior managerial employees reported that they worked longer than their contracted hours. Thus, as in Shopwell and Cellbank, managerial employees in the councils tended to work longer hours than lower-level council employees.

[7] In CCC flexitime was something of a bone of contention at the time of our interviews. Management argued that flexitime had fallen into abuse, as some employees were using it to engineer regular days off, causing problems for other workers. However, the eventual reform of the system did not result in any serious reduction of flexitime hours.

Discussion and conclusions

In this chapter, we have focused primarily on the impact of flexible working on employment careers in three different contexts (other issues relating to employment careers will be explored in subsequent chapters). The three organisations drew on rather different segments of the labour market and, in broad outline, the people working in them had rather different employment/family trajectories. In Shopwell, levels of education/qualification among employees were relatively low, and Shopwell employees – both men and women – had had rather fragmentary employment experience. Cellbank employees usually had middling levels of educational qualifications. Despite the upheavals in the finance industry, the majority of Cellbank employees had been with Cellbank for all of their working lives, although some women had interrupted their employment in order to care for children. The Council employees had the highest average level of qualification, and many were long-service employees. However, this was by no means universally the case, and many interviewees (particularly in CCC) had diverse career paths. However – and in some contrast to Shopwell – Council employees had been mobile into and out of reasonably good and secure employment.

As we have seen in the introduction to this chapter, it may be argued that one positive consequence of the supposed decline of the 'organisational' career and the development of the individualised, 'boundaryless' career is that the impact of broken career paths and flexible working that have long characterised women's employment might now be less important as far as employment careers are concerned.

In general, however, our matches indicated that people who had not changed their hours or worked flexibly had done better, in career terms, than those who had not done so. In part, this finding will reflect the cumulative impact of past practices – such as Cellbank women having been unable to take a career break or return to part-time work at the same grade – that have now been changed (as we have seen in the example of Flora and Peggy). Other factors (besides career breaks and flexible working) will also have had an impact on career development. Individual motivations and competencies will be very important, as will the particular (and changing) nature of career opportunities in the organisations themselves.

Despite individual complaints, most interviewees appreciated that employers did now make efforts to be family friendly.

Flora (Cellbank): "Maternity leave and paternity leave now, offering part-time contracts.... We've got emergency carers' leave."

Ursula (CCC): "I do think it is a good employer. It does genuinely try to be flexible."

Nevertheless, as we have seen, the hours worked by managers put considerable limits on their flexibility in practice, particularly in Shopwell and Cellbank. Thus the advantages of family-friendliness tended to be enjoyed mainly by those in lower-level employment, and individuals wishing to move into managerial positions had to be prepared to work the hours required. Considerable publicity has been given to the 'long hours culture' that keeps women out of the very topmost jobs, but our evidence suggests that the necessity to work long hours in fact takes effect at much lower levels of the managerial and supervisory hierarchy[8].

Although our interviews can in no sense be taken to represent a 'sample', it did seem to be the case that there were more examples of flexible working among women in the higher-grade levels in the Councils. Of the 14 women interviewed who were above grade 4-5, six worked part time. However, these women tended to be in specialist and/or professional jobs, rather than in the line management 'mainstream'[9]. This finding echoes previous research that has demonstrated that women (and men) with specialist qualifications and competencies are enabled to work more flexibly than women (and men) in managerial positions (Butler and Savage, 1996; Crompton and Harris, 1998).

Recent changes in career structures mean that long, unbroken service with a single organisation is less significant for career development than it has been in the past, particularly in sectors such as banking. It is also possible to return to employment after a career break and rebuild an organisational career, as, for example, Peggy (Cellbank) and Janine (Council) had done. Nevertheless, absences from employment will still have an impact, particularly if they are relatively extensive. We may illustrate this by taking another example from Cellbank. Both Louise and Abigail joined Cellbank after 'A' level. Louise (now aged 50) had had a five-year childrearing break and had then returned to work part time. After three years working part time, she moved to full time and reached grade 3 in her forties. Abigail, like Louise, had two children in her twenties, and has returned to part

---

[8] See *The Guardian*, 13 June 2002, 'Women struggle to join £100K club'.

[9] Because these jobs are specialised, precise information has not been given for fear of breaching confidentiality.

time work but not taken a childrearing break. She is now 30, and is also grade 3.

The stories of Louise and Abigail are of women of two different generations, with different work–family histories and operating within different sets of organisational policies. Whether Abigail will progress further in the bank, despite her shift to part-time employment, is yet to be seen. At the present time, however, she is relatively pessimistic as to her prospects, unless she returns to full-time work:

> Abigail (Cellbank): "I admit I could [go] further, but I'm high up here anyway. But it's because I can't come back full time. If I came back full time then I could go a lot further, but I haven't got the childcare facilities to do that."

3

Work–life integration, organisational policies and organisational cultures

Introduction: what kinds of organisation have positive work–life policies?

The most up-to-date quantitative account of work–life balance policies is by Dex and Smith (2002). This report analysed the 1997/98 Workplace and Employer Relations (WERS) data set, which includes interviews with managers and workers in over 2,191 workplaces and questionnaires from 28,323 employees from these same workplaces, representing approximately three quarters of all employees in employment in Britain in 1998. Multivariate analysis was used to identify the workplace characteristics associated with the presence of substantial 'family-friendly' policies. These are:

- larger organisations and establishments;
- public sector;
- lower degrees of competition;
- recognised unions;
- human resources and good performance;
- high commitment management practices;
- more involvement of employees in decision making;
- stronger equal opportunities policies;
- larger proportions of women in the workforce;
- highly educated workforce using discretion.

Our four case study organisations, therefore, were characterised by a number of the factors associated with the presence of 'family-friendly' policies and, indeed, such policies were, to varying extents, positively promoted in all of the organisations studied. They were relatively large organisations, they had extensive human resources, equal opportunities policies, high commitment management practices, and a substantial proportion of women in the workforce. The Councils, of course, were in the public sector, and in the Councils (and to some extent in Cellbank) the workforce was highly educated. However, as Dex and Smith note, although survey data is essential in describing the broad contours and scope of policies, it does not "generate discursive accounts of employer practices and workplace cultures and their impact on family-friendly policies" (2002, p 25). In this chapter, we will draw on our interviews to examine more closely the interaction between these interrelated topics. First, we will explore the topic of organisational culture.

Organisational culture

Within the managerial literature, the concept of 'culture' has achieved a wide currency following the impact of Peters and Waterman's influential book (1982) relating to the positive impact of the development of a 'culture of excellence'. It draws on the idea that "organisations work best where members' and organisations' beliefs, attitudes and goals are mutually compatible" (Grint, 1991, p 126) and involves the effective management of symbols, meanings, beliefs and values. In brief, the aim is to make the goals and objectives of the organisation the personal goals and objectives of the employees themselves (du Gay, 1996, p 61). Thus the aim is to 'work on' the individual, to develop the 'entrepreneurial self' (Rose, 1993). As Thompson and Warhurst have suggested, it has been argued that "we do not have 'hands' in today's organisations. The popular view is that organisations are opting, by choice or necessity, to engage with hearts and minds instead" (1998, p 1).

Du Gay (1996) and Rose (1993) have laid a considerable emphasis on the 'individualising' element in the management of culture literature. They draw extensive parallels between strategic efforts to build 'enterprise culture(s)' and the political impact and effects of economic liberalism since the 1980s. It is not difficult to find organisational examples here of the growth of individualised pay scales and (as we have seen) individualised promotion systems, of individual and interteam competitiveness being consciously developed within organisations, and so on.

However, the positive development and encouragement of the entrepreneurial self together with organisational commitment can cut across other aspects of existence that are difficult to fit within a market-oriented, competitive culture. In particular, it may affect the work of caregiving which has conventionally been regarded as governed by ideals of responsibility and altruism love and affection, rather than market forces. Indeed, in an influential case study, Hochschild (1997) has documented how, with the increasing development and application of these managerial techniques, there is a danger that 'work becomes home and home becomes work', to the detriment of family life. That is, in her example (of a company with excellent family-friendly policies), efforts to build the employees' identification with the company had the effect of seriously eroding 'family' time.

In practice, the term 'culture' has a loose and wide application and would seem to be used as a general term to describe attempts to build organisational beliefs and value systems. In two of the organisations studied – Shopwell and Cellbank – strategies of cultural change were explicitly linked to attempts to develop individualised, entrepreneurial cultures within the organisations. The demands of customer-led service involved a shift in control strategies. A more trusting, communicative and consultative form of management was inaugurated, together with the development of a culture of 'responsibilisation'. As we have seen, in both Shopwell and Cellbank, one aspect of these cultural developments has been the development of individualised schemes for promotion where "the apparent aim is to put the responsibility for generating promotional opportunities in the hands of the employee" (Grimshaw et al, 2001, p 49).

A deliberate strategy of cultural change had not been as explicitly developed in either of the Councils. In any case, as we have seen in our previous chapter, the Councils were less monolithic and it would have been difficult to develop a uniform culture across all departments. Politically, the Councils had different recent histories: Sheffield has been a Left Labour council, Canterbury/Kent radical Tory/Liberal Democrat. Nevertheless, in both Councils many interviewees shared an ethos of public service.

Organisational cultures, careers and working hours

As we have seen, Dex and Smith (2002) have found high commitment management practices to be positively associated with the presence of family-friendly employment policies. It might be argued, therefore, that this turn of the wheel has brought with it the beginnings of a resolution of the growing tensions between employment and family life that were brought into play in earlier attempts to develop entrepreneurial cultures, in which commitment to the job was emphasised above all. Indeed (and most optimistically), with the growth of family-friendly policies the goals of the individual might become the goals of the organisation, rather than the other way round.

However, organisational case studies focusing on family-friendly policies and their use have been less optimistic. As Lewis (1997, p 18) has argued, positive work–life and/or family-friendly policies co-exist uneasily with other organisational values, such as those that put the major value on employees who do not allow family commitments to intrude in their working lives, and put in long hours in the workplace. She identifies two major barriers to a culture change in a family-friendly direction: subjective senses of entitlement, and organisational discourses of time. In her research, family-friendly provisions were seen as being 'perks' rather than a basic right (women were more likely than men to feel 'entitled' to these provisions but less likely to feel 'entitled' to a career), and long hours working was seen as a measure of organisational commitment.

Lewis' findings are echoed by Hojgaard's (1997) research. In Scandinavia, where Hojgaard carried out her research, welfare state policies are directly aimed at softening or ameliorating the contradictions between family and employment. In particular, they encouraged men to take on a more active involvement in family life. However, her case studies (of three organisations) suggest that organisational career cultures in practice render this impossible:

It is a commonly held view by the men in all three companies that career and family are incompatible... In the ministry it is the fight for the good and prestigious work tasks and the ability to be available at all times that are complicated by family obligations.... In the medical firm it is the size of the workload necessary for pursuing a career that will hurt the family, and in the bank it is the feeling of not living up to the norms prescribed for a serious career maker that is felt to be the obstacle. (1997, p 256)

It is apparent, therefore, that in most, if not all, organisational contexts, 'putting in the hours' is seen to be an integral element of career development, even to the lower rungs of the organisational hierarchy. As we have seen in the last chapter, the necessity to work long hours was widely seen as a disincentive as far as going for promotion to manager was concerned in both Shopwell and Cellbank, and in the Councils managers on higher grades also worked relatively long hours.

Thus people wanting to develop an organisational career are likely to work long hours. This would also seem to be the case in countries with shorter working hours than Britain (for example, in Denmark, where Hojgaard carried out her research, full-time weekly working hours [men and women] average 39.3 hours). In low-paid jobs, people will work longer hours in order to increase their total earnings; this was certainly a motivation as far as some non-managerial Shopwell employees were concerned. It would be acknowledged that full-time employees in Britain work relatively long hours (Fagan, 2001). For example, the 2000 Labour Force Survey reports average hours worked per week (men and women combined) in the UK as 43.6, as compared to a 39.6 EU 11 average. Thus we frequently find reference to the prevalence of a 'long hours' working culture in Britain. However, to what extent may it be argued that in Britain there is a 'long hours culture' in a *normative* sense – that is, people

feel that they *ought* to work long hours and that they will be less valued in an organisational context if they do not. Alternatively, to what extent is a 'long hours culture' a consequence of the amount of work required by employers because of the way in which the work is organised and/or the low wages that are paid?

It would be difficult to disentangle completely the different sources of long hours working, not least because they will overlap with each other. However, there can be little doubt that many of our interviewees took the view that a major cause of long hours working – and of difficulties in implementing family-friendly policies more generally – was the tight levels of staffing in the organisations concerned. As we concluded in the ECFFEP report, (Yeandle et al, 2002) 'lean' organisations are not particularly family friendly.

Market and service pressures in the three organisations and their impact on work–life policies

Organisational restructuring and delayering, as noted above, has been a core element in new managerial techniques. The managerial rationale for such reorganisations is summed up in the widely cited phrase: 'Work smarter, not harder' (Womack et al, 1990). In theory, taking out managerial and supervisory layers and the creation of the 'lean' organisation, together with the generation of a culture of 'responsibilisation', will increase organisational efficiency. Thus the same objectives will be achieved at less cost. However, many of our interviewees took the view that 'lean' staffing not only increased the pressures of work – that is, they worked harder, not smarter – but also made the implementation of family-friendly policies more problematic because of the difficulty of providing cover for absent colleagues.

These difficulties were particularly acute for people whose jobs were concerned with direct service delivery. Individuals working on particular projects (for example, an environmental audit) found it easier to be flexible, as they were able to make up lost working time without affecting other people. As Bill (Cellbank, working on a project implementing a new system) put it: "the staffing being reduced in branches, they haven't got enough hours in the day.... I saw it last week. I went to a branch to work-shadow a branch manager, and he was there until 7 o'clock every night. Just to get his paperwork up straight. Just to ensure that he was there with his targets. Just to be ready for the next day. And all that is taken without any overtime or anything like that.... I am lucky in the job that I do in that I can take that time off if I want to. I know it's going to be very difficult to go back into the branch network because the flexibility is not there."[10]

The extent to which employees were responsible for service delivery and/or project work varied within the organisations we studied. In Shopwell, employees were largely concerned with service delivery although, as we have seen in the example of Grace in the last chapter, it was largely the managers who took on the ultimate responsibility. In Cellbank, service delivery in personal financial services (where we carried out our interviews) was also a priority. The situation was complicated by the fact that many of the bank branches were relatively small, thus leading to difficulties in providing cover for absent staff. The Councils included more of a mix of service deliverers and project workers. Both Councils also operated flexitime systems, and many interviewees were able to use the flexibility to balance their employment and caring responsibilities. Nevertheless, Council employees in libraries, leisure centres, care homes, and so on, faced very similar problems in providing a continuity of service, as did Shopwell and Cellbank employees.

In Cellbank, interviewees were acutely aware of the problems that their absence might cause for colleagues.

Jenny: "I've got a problem at home with my daughter, there are certain days here when there are only the two of you. And you are torn between doing the right thing for your colleague and doing the right thing for your daughter. And your daughter's got to come first. But you know it's going to put your colleague in a very difficult position. And it makes it more stressful."

Her comments are echoed by Vicky and Beth:

Vicky: "You have mothers who want to take a carers' day because a child is not well, but a lot of the time those people are cashiers and personal bankers and they know the state it will leave you in, so they will find another way and someone else will look after their child."

Beth: "It depends on [my daughter]; when she was ill we were short staffed on some days so I couldn't take time off, well I could but I wouldn't but the last time she was off was on a Friday and we're not short staffed so it wasn't so bad. I always try to avoid taking time off when we're short staffed; I feel like I'm letting colleagues down."

Thus, although the family-friendly policies introduced by Cellbank were known of and appreciated, many argued that staff shortages made them very difficult to put into practice:

Abigail: "[The bank] forget about those who are left in the branch, they don't necessarily replace that person. They are good to the person who is actually off but they forget about everyone who is left to cover."

Poppy: "I mean, the bank plant ideas into our heads but then don't help see it through. If we haven't got the resources to cover when someone wants to go on an employment or career break, how can we see it through?"

Another point made was that bank targets still had to be met even if staff took legitimate advantage of family-friendly options.

Vicky: "We still have to achieve the same level of results. You can't say I didn't achieve that or I had a queue out the door, I'm sorry, because so and so had a carers' day. That's not acceptable. You have to still achieve the same level.... And it's down to us to manage that, at my level. It doesn't go any further up."

Philip: "In the sort of environment we're working in, which is very much target-driven, if you are – it sounds ridiculous – on carers leave, that's a day you've lost that you don't get back, you're not there to do

---

[10] A parallel may be drawn here with the flexible professionals discussed in the last chapter.

anything towards achieving your targets. You're playing catch-up all the time."

Cellbank employees who worked extra hours were given time off in lieu, although some complained that they were unable to take it up. Shopwell employees were paid overtime although, as in Cellbank, managers worked overtime without pay. Shopwell interviewees did complain about problems with staffing.

Jean: "Like [all] supermarkets, it's just run on bone. If someone does go down, yes it does tip the boat a bit."

Debbie: "They don't seem to keep their checkout staff. They are always leaving. People don't seem to be staying. With leave, when you put in for holiday or whatever, they haven't got people to cover you. They panic that we can't have the time off, but then what are you going to do? You are only going to go sick."

However, Shopwell employees were less likely than those in Cellbank to think that their colleagues would suffer if they were absent; rather, the gap was filled by the managers.

Barry: "I have worked 70 hours in the past. I work at home. I put in the hours when I need to. That's part of being a manager but you're never really asked to."

Martin: "It's all cost, isn't it? To make it family friendly you need to employ more managers. You need almost a couple of floating managers that if one has to go early that manager can fit in, but it is cost, isn't it?"[11]

Some jobs in the Councils were concerned with direct service delivery and were therefore subject to pressures in relation to cover:

Molly: "When I'm there I'm in charge of the building, and it needs somebody of my level to be there. If I have to go for any reason, it means somebody else coming in to cover my shift."

In both Councils, reorganisations and cutbacks had led to shortages of staff.

Isobel: "We are so pushed and they have cut the staffing levels right down. To get the work done a lot of people stay late. We are on flexitime whereby you build up time and you can take the day off. But I do know a lot of people who don't get the chance to take their days off, purely because they want to keep on top of the work."

Nevertheless, in general, employees in the Councils did have more job autonomy and were able to take advantage of flexitime:

Olivia: "[My son] had to go into hospital earlier this year … and there was no problem having some time off. We just cover for each other, basically … because I'm flexible and I had a date in advance, I just said to [my line manager], when she was doing the rota, can I have the time off. So I just didn't work. I worked extra hours the week before and the week after. That worked out well."

Pressures to work long hours, therefore, may not be so much culturally required or expected (although they often were in the case of managers), but may be a byproduct of the way in which work is organised, particularly work that is concerned with direct service delivery. Particularly in the case of Cellbank, it may be suggested that different aspects of organisational policies tended to work against each other. On the one hand, Cellbank wished to promote family-friendly policies as part of its strategy to be the 'employer of choice'; on the other hand, policies designed to make the organisation more competitive worked against the implementation of family-friendly entitlements.

Sense of entitlement to work–life policies

Lewis (1997) has argued that an important cultural element working against the implementation of family-friendly policies is that they are generally seen as 'perks' – particularly for women – rather than as entitlements. We have attempted to explore this topic by asking

---

11 Shopwell are attempting to reduce managerial working hours, and have introduced a 'friends and families' rota for managers that gives one weekend off in three.

our interviewees whether they ever felt guilty about taking time off for family reasons. Many people – both men and women – said they would not feel guilty, largely because they felt that they kept to their side of the 'effort bargain' with their employers, and/or because they would be able to make up their work in any case (this applied more to people doing project work than service delivery work).

Scott (Cellbank): "No, not at all. I don't feel that I owe the bank a living. I think they owe me because I have given them 17 of the best years of my life. I wouldn't think twice about it."

Derek (CCC): "No, because I know that I work a lot more hours than they pay me for and I would make the work up. The fact is, the work will get done."

Ursula (CCC): "I would never feel guilty. It's a rare occurrence that I need to take time off, and I put the hours in anyway. They've had more than their pound of flesh from me."

Poppy (Cellbank): "It doesn't affect me. I work a lot on my own and if necessary if I'm off sick I just work longer hours to make the time up."

A minority said they would feel guilty because "that's the way I am": that is, they felt they had a particularly strong work ethic:

Kevin (Shopwell): "I feel guilty because I've been brought up never to have time off. Especially my dad, he never allowed us to have time off school and it rubs off on our kids too."

Most of those who said they would feel guilty, however, were concerned about the impact of their absence on their colleagues:

Lorna (SCC): "I feel guilty. Once I was involved in a meeting and I had to go and collect my daughter from school because she was ill. It means that there's more pressure on other colleagues who are at work so you feel bad."

Charles (CCC): "Yes, I do. I have done in the past, especially with the team because

we do work so closely. If we are involved in a project and I know I'm going to have to disappear ... and I knew I had left them in the middle of something and I felt I should be there really."

Jenny (Cellbank): "Yes, I do, for the people here, for my closest work colleagues."

Cassie (Cellbank): "I feel very guilty ... but it's just the way I am. I know that if I'm off there'll be no replacement and they'll be short staffed all day."

These kinds of answers suggest that if employees (men and women) lacked a sense of entitlement, it was largely in respect of their workplace colleagues rather than their employing organisation (Phillips et al, 2002; Yeandle et al, 2002). Thus, even though new managerial techniques in general seek to promote a culture of individualisation, a collective feeling of responsibility to colleagues would seem to remain important, and might even interfere with the take-up of family-friendly policies.

Employee views on work–life policies

Besides the question of organisational culture, one of the aims of our research was to explore whether recent changes in emphasis relating to carer-friendly working arrangements had made an impact on employees' perceptions of these arrangements, and the likelihood of their taking them up. We asked all of our interviewees whether or not they considered their organisation to be family-friendly: that is, how easy their employer made it for people to balance their work and family responsibilities. Most people were aware of most policies (we should remember that our interviewees included a greater than average proportion of people with caring responsibilities), and most people – although in each organisation there were important reservations – thought that things had improved:

Louise (Cellbank): "Yes, I would, because they brought in the carers' days. And if there is a problem, they do appreciate that you've got families. And they are very accommodating to part-timers for their family needs."

Hannah (Cellbank): "[They have] quite a good range of policies. When your child starts school at first you can have half a day off. Maternity leave is good. You're not penalised if you have a family. There is carers' leave.... When I get married I get an extra week unpaid leave, it's all designed to help you."

Nevertheless, although these improvements were widely recognised, others at Cellbank felt that wider company pressures interfered:

Cliff (Cellbank): "Overall in principle they are, but at the grass-roots level there is a shortage of staff and this puts on more pressure and they don't always consider the family implications of this. The policies are there but at the end of the day there are too many individuals with too many targets to meet so you lose sight of the family issues."

Vicky (Cellbank): "No, it's not. They think they are but they're not really. They do think they are and they spend a lot of time talking about it.... Because the whole thing of it is that they rely on people's conscience for everything so that people won't be off sick."

Peggy (Cellbank): "The bank want to be seen as a flexible employer to suit the bank but also the employees. As a whole they try to do the right things. They have flexitime but it's difficult with kids to take time off work. Part time is possible but the higher you get in the organisation the more committed you have to be and part-time work is not always equated with commitment."

Both Councils (Sheffield in particular) had good policies, but to a larger extent than in Cellbank and Shopwell, their effectiveness was seen to depend to a considerable extent on managerial discretion. As Derek (CCC) put it: "I would distinguish between different bits of the council. I think any council is in reality a series of departments which to a large extent do their own things. There are central policies in place, but it's how they are interpreted and that depends very much upon the managers". Marcia (SCC) echoes his comments: "It depends. The council on the whole is, but it depends on your line

manager. Mine hasn't got any kids and so is not very helpful".

Thus there is considerable variability in the implementation of policies in both Councils, as illustrated by Olga's (CCC) experience: "They are quite supportive. It depends who you work for, what the boss is like, basically. My boss, five years ago he had a child, and he has become remarkably sympathetic to me. That was very helpful, let me reorganise my.... But other sections, they won't get anything really, won't get any help at all". Nevertheless, as Agatha (SCC) summed up the situation: "Flexitime is good. Most people have families and young children and it helps. They are good at maternity leave policy. We have certain guidelines and it depends on the managers. If they want staff to be flexible they have to be flexible with the staff. We are encouraged by HR to be family friendly".

Shopwell offers a wide range of family-friendly policies and extensive opportunities for flexible working. As Katrina said: "They are very good. They get paternity leave. There's a bloke here who doesn't work during school holidays – because his wife has got a very good job – he looks after the children while his wife carries on working. You can get grandma leave. There are quite good things". Charlotte had benefited directly: "They helped me when I went on maternity leave. They provided me with information at home. I got straight back into the job I was doing when I came back which is good. If you need time off because your child is ill they'd let you go straight away, I think".

However, these advantages were largely experienced at the basic employee level. As Craig, a manager, said:

"They are family friendly on the outside as far as maternity leave, paternity leave, those things are family friendly. There are lots of things there that they are trying to improve. Flexibility for shop-floor workers, yes. Family friendly for shop-floor workers, yes. Family friendly for managers, to a point ... no ... then of course really you've got to make a commitment to the company."

Fiona, another Shopwell manager, makes a similar argument:

"They are quite flexible in their approach to contract hours, especially for shop-floor workers. They do work around you, so yes, they are [family friendly]. So on the shop-floor, yes.... You know when you go into management that you will be working some evenings, some early mornings. It's not just a straightforward 9 to 5 job."

Discussion and conclusions

In this chapter, we have explored the way in which work–life and family-friendly policies are mediated by the organisational cultures of our case study organisations. The notion of organisational culture is complex and difficult to specify precisely, but one feature common to all of the organisations studied was that 'career' positions would mean working longer hours. As we have already demonstrated in Chapter 2, promotion to even the lower levels of management carries with it the expectation that individuals have the organisational commitment to work longer hours if required, and people sometimes have to demonstrate this commitment in advance by long hours working. Most people in non-career positions, and/or who were not interested in a career (this included some professionals), did not work beyond their contracted hours unless they needed the overtime income.

In contrast, the situation in relation to flexible working, and taking time off for family reasons (such as carers' days), varied. Flexibility in Shopwell was very extensive and the company went to considerable effort to accommodate people's requirements. However, much of this flexibility was unpaid, and, as James put it:

"They have this [long holiday] leave after Christmas when they are trying to cut back on hours; it's unpaid holidays to cut the wages bill down. The leave they have is mainly unpaid leave."

Cellbank had paid carers' leave but, as we have seen, people often felt they could not take advantage of it because of the need to meet targets, as well as not letting colleagues down because of the difficulties in providing cover in the branches. A similar situation prevailed in some Council departments, although, in general, work flexibility was easier to achieve in the

Councils because of the presence of flexitime. Flexitime, however, cannot be easily introduced (or used) if service cover has to be maintained at fixed times and places. In CCC, flexitime was not available above grade 10.

People's hours of work and whether they work flexibly, therefore, are determined not merely by organisational policies together with individual career aspirations, but also by the nature of the work to be carried out as well as by the way in which this work is organised and resourced. If service cover has to be provided, then the employee concerned may not actually *want* to stay on at work, or turn up to work when their child is ill, but simply feel unable to do otherwise. Similarly, if levels of staffing are tight, then policies to which the employee feels perfectly entitled may not be taken advantage of because employees wish to protect their colleagues. In the Councils, managerial discretion appeared to be particularly important in shaping the way in which work–life policies are implemented.

In each organisation, therefore, there were particular features that impacted on the effectiveness of the family-friendly policies available. That being said, there was also an appreciation of the new policies that had been introduced and many thought that the situation was getting better:

Sheila (Cellbank): "Cellbank have as a whole, they have got better. They now provide carers' days. My team leader, she is quite flexible as well. She has got a young daughter as well, so she does try to be very flexible if you need to leave early or if my child is poorly. She's flexible with that sort of thing. But sometimes there's the odd individual that is more committed to the bank than perhaps other people. Perhaps they put their work life before their family. But yes, Cellbank as a whole, they have got a lot better. They are trying to be family friendly."

4

Women, men, caring and careers

In this chapter, we focus on the way in which our interviewees managed their employment, careers and family lives. In the first part of the chapter, we will discuss how parenting responsibilities impinged on attitudes to career development. In the second section, we will discuss how families with employed parents managed childcare, and how these responsibilities for parenting are changing and developing.

Careers and caring

In Chapter 2, we have demonstrated that people who had not taken a career break or moved to part-time work had done better, in career terms, than those who had done so. Women had been more likely to take a break and/or work flexibly than men. Few would disagree with the general statement that caring responsibilities, particularly for children, bring with them problems as far as individual career development is concerned. Our interviewees were no exception here, as is demonstrated in this answer to a direct question about career development in the organisation:

Megan (Shopwell): "I want to go further in the company and become a manager. It's quite easy to be a manager but I won't do it straight away. The children are too young and you need to work long hours at work. In two or three years I will want to do it."

These extracts echo some of the themes developed in Chapter 2 – that is, that developing a career will mean working full time, as well as long hours of work. However, some interviewees (men and women) say that they have nevertheless *chosen* to give priority to their family lives:

Dennis (Cellbank): "It's very much a choice between family life or work life, and I've chosen the balance which is why I think I'm in a job (rather than a career). My boss is 29 and I don't think he sees his child from one week to the next.... I couldn't do that. But then he's driving a flash car and earning considerably more than I am. That's the choice he has made."

Lorna (Council): "Children have changed that, I have to put them first and realise that I can't be too concerned about getting in a better position at the moment. I wouldn't want a job with too much responsibility because it would be too hard juggling home life and work."

Thus it might be argued – as, for example, Hakim (2000) has done – that the major factor that explains varying work–life trajectories as far as men and women are concerned is the different distribution of *preferences* between the sexes. In brief, Hakim argues that three groups of women may be identified (family-centred, work-centred, and 'adaptive'), and that in two of these groups (family-centred and adaptive) women are less likely to pursue a career than men because they prefer to give their families priority. The position we take here is that preferences *are* important, but it is of equal – if not more – importance to understand and explain the context within which these preferences are developed.

We have attempted to capture the issue of preferences by asking interviewees whether or not they thought of themselves as a 'career person'[12]. Our responses were extremely mixed, reflecting differences in age, organisational position, and family circumstances – that is, personal and employment contexts – among the people we interviewed. Women were less likely to say that they thought of themselves as a 'career person' than men, and were more likely to cite family reasons and/or childcare responsibilities as a reason for not wanting a career.

Molly (Council): "Not now. I did at one time, but not any more ... now I'm not ambitious at all. I wouldn't want to be the manager. I'm not interested. I'm happy in my job. My family is everything now."

Katrina (Shopwell): "No, not really because I got married and I went into the jobs which suited my daughter."

Women in Shopwell (Irene, Katrina, Charlotte) were somewhat less likely to be interested in a career and more likely to say that it was 'just a job' – probably a reflection of both the actual level of career opportunities available at Shopwell as well as the level of qualifications among Shopwell employees. However, other women were ambitious and had actively developed their careers.

Ida: "Yes, I do ... I think I've done exceedingly well, actually. When I started with Canterbury City Council; well, I didn't start with the Council, I started with an offshoot.... So I started there in an administration role, and because I had a very dynamic boss then, she encouraged me enormously. I progressed. She put me through my study."

Zoe (Cellbank): "Yes. I like a challenge. I like to set a goal and a challenge but once I get there I get a bit bored and need to do something else."

Although the relative emphasis on careers and family differed between men and women, in that more women than men explicitly placed their families 'before' their employment careers, the nature of the rationales given by men and women in answers to questions about careers were very similar. Organisational changes were seen as having made career progression more difficult. In Cellbank, both men and women thought that recent restructuring had made things worse, and cutbacks and restrictions on expenditure were seen as hampering the potential for career development within the Councils (see Chapter 3).

Kerry (Cellbank): "Yes [is a 'career' person], because I enjoy my work and I want to do well in it ... the availability for training and promotion upwards is quite limited still because upon the restructure, whereas when you first started at the bank there were lots of different avenues to go in each job, and then quite a lot of ways to move up, now ways are quite restricted because there aren't the jobs available ... before the restructuring there would be seven or eight different jobs they could do within that grade [G3] so those jobs have all either been dispersed or been centralised. There is not the availability of them any more. Different skills are needed now from 10 or 15 years ago ... the avenues are very limited now."

Mervyn: "At SCC you could get promotion up until five years ago but not now.... The local authority are reducing costs, service departments want to cut services or outsource departments which leads to a reduction of staff. We had 130 people in this department 10 years ago, now we have got 30."

In summary, as we have seen in this chapter as well as in previous chapters, individuals who wish to pursue an organisational career will have to work longer hours in order to achieve promotion, and will usually have to work full time. People do make choices and among our interviewees many people, particularly women, had chosen to give their families priority over promotion opportunities and/or career building. However, it is important always to remember that choices are (a) made from the opportunities that are available and (b) in the light of perceived

---

[12] Given the stated objectives of the research, of which our interviewees were fully aware, this could be criticised as being a leading question. We also asked people if they were happy with their employment career.

constraints. The opportunities available to an individual will depend on both their individual characteristics (for example, their level of qualification), as well as the opportunities available within the organisation, and indeed in the labour market more generally. In the context of our discussion, constraints will include the demands and requirements of other 'work', particularly caring work.

The question of choice is a complex issue. Individuals who have not been particularly successful in employment career terms might well rationalise their lack of success by citing their family responsibilities. Prevailing normative assumptions make it easier for women to cite family responsibilities as a reason for not pursuing or achieving a career although, as we have seen, men did do so as well. It is important to remember that although the work of caring is gender 'coded', in that women will conventionally be assumed to be the carers, if men have to care, then their careers will be similarly affected.

> Greg (Cellbank): "I started out with a career in mind but things got in the way. I used to have to look after them both [parents] and get home as soon as possible to look after them. In those days you had to take the banking exams and you had to do it at night but because I had to look after my parents it got in the way of my career."

Here the potential for conflict between caring and career aspirations is apparent. Nevertheless, are there any signs of change – in particular, how did our interviewees manage their caring responsibilities, and is there any evidence that men are assuming more of them?

Employment, careers and family life: responsibilities past and present

Both careers and caring stretch over a lifetime, so we asked not just about caring in the present, but also about caring in the past. Sixty-six of our interviewees had a child aged under 16 but, in total, 108 of our interviewees had children. We have noted that the level of caring responsibilities among our respondents was high, and 31 of our interviewees had caring responsibilities (for parents, disabled relatives,

and so on) at the time of the interview; 13 of these also had children under the age of 16. A further seven interviewees had had caring responsibilities other than childcare in the past.

Changes over time in both men's but more particularly in women's expectations of employment and family life are absolutely crucial to our understanding of changing patterns of care for children. In Chapter 1 we emphasised that, in Britain, women only began returning to employment after childbirth in substantial numbers from the 1980s. The timing of this trend was very noticeable among the women we interviewed. Of the 31 women whose youngest child was 17 or over, all had taken an employment break or changed their working hours. Twenty-nine had taken a break, and only two had returned to work part time without taking a break[13].

> Daphne (Cellbank): "In those days you didn't work. You left work. There was no maternity leave, or anything like that. You left work to have a family and you couldn't go back."

> Irene (Shopwell): "Then it was just what you did. They didn't seem to work a lot like they do now. Now it's back to work soon after. When I had mine it wasn't the thing. You left work and that was it."

In some contrast, of the 30 women whose youngest child was 10 or under, only three had had an employment break, 21 had changed their working hours, and six had carried on working full time. Thus, as far as our older interviewees (men and women) are concerned, our understanding of the nature of their work–life integration over the period of childrearing can be fairly straightforward: men went out to work, women looked after the children. Among younger interviewees (and those with younger children), however, the situation is much more complex. Not only are more women with relatively young children in employment, but more men with young children are likely to have

---

[13] Of the 11 women whose youngest child was aged 11-16, eight had taken a break, two had returned to work part time, and one had not taken a break or changed her hours. These figures are not representative, but they suggest that the major change in behaviour has taken place over the last decade.

wives and partners in employment. Our discussion of balancing work and family life, therefore, will focus on families and parents with children under the age of 10.

Families with non-adult children: responsibilities for parenting

As we have noted above, in the case of interviewees with adult children, the model of parenting that predominated was the one associated with the 'male breadwinner' model of employment and family life: the man was employed, the woman did the caring. Of course, there have always been exceptions to this rule, but nevertheless it is reasonable to make this generalisation. Our questions about childcare, and a partner's involvement in childcare, revealed a complex range of solutions among the parents of young children as far as the balance of responsibility for childcare was concerned.

All children have two parents. Although there were a number of separated (that is, lone) parents among our interviewees, our respondents' descriptions of childcare arrangements suggest that most parents take caring responsibility for children at some time or other, even though the partnership itself may not be a lasting one. Changes in family circumstances mean that caring responsibilities can vary quite considerably over time:

Sophie (Shopwell): "He was involved in childcare until she was four when we split up. He worked in the afternoons and would look after her in the mornings and I would start work early and then take over."

Bill (Cellbank): "I'm not living with my daughter's mother.... Obviously I have her at weekends, half-terms and school holidays. I was more involved when she was younger; I would take more time off from work. When she was born I took a month's unpaid parental leave. After that I was quite flexible in that I would take two or possibly three days off a month, from my holiday leave."

Although, therefore, we will identify parental strategy 'clusters' among our interviewees, we should nevertheless always be conscious of the fact that these are fluid and shifting, and will often represent a relatively short-term or temporary state of affairs.

Most children live in heterosexual families. We can think of parenting strategies, therefore, as being located along a continuum of largely female (mother's) responsibility at one pole, and largely male (father's) responsibility at the other. Among the parents of younger children, there were many families where women reported that they still took the major responsibility for childcare. For example, Abigail (Cellbank), when asked about her partner's involvement, replied "zilch".

Rita (Council): "If anyone was ill, it was me that took the days off. I liaised with the nanny, prepared the paper work. Organising the kids, I did it, it was all me. He wasn't really involved."

Other women were less concerned about the extent of their responsibilities:

Shauna (Council): "I'm fine about it. I like it like that. I do the vast majority of the caring at home and he does things if he's around. It's just a man thing."

In many instances, men's working hours were cited as the major reason for lack of sharing of childcare:

Emma (Cellbank): "Well, he's away from the house from 7.30 am to 6 pm. He's only there in the evenings."

Alec (Council): "When I worked in retail it was fairly demanding, and I used to leave home at 7 am and leave work at 6 pm. I used to do what I could at weekends. My ex-wife did most of the hard work."

We may describe these kinds of arrangements as *female dominant parenting* (or *separate parenting*; see La Valle et al, 2002). Other fathers contributed more, although their partners worked part time thus doing more childcare. Such arrangements may be described as *joint female biased parenting*.

Cassie (Cellbank): "On the days that I work, he goes into work later so he can take the kids to school and to nursery. He has more flexibility at work than I do. All childcare activities are shared between us now, when he's got the time. I work part time so I'm there more than he is."

Scott (Cellbank): "I would never consider, if my wife was working and I was off, to call my mother-in-law in because it's quality time, isn't it. I don't spend enough time with him because I'm working five days a week and she's working two, so we share it equally."

Among the younger families, therefore, on average mothers still do more childcare than fathers. Nevertheless, help from fathers can be absolutely crucial when both parents are in employment. This is particularly apparent when the jobs of one or both parents involve unusual or unsocial hours. Indeed, parents often structure their jobs in order to accommodate childcare. This pattern may be described as *shift parenting*. In these instances, fathers often share childcare equally with mothers[14].

Isobel (Council): "... when I first went back to work he used to do shiftwork. He would be around in the morning so every other week he would look after the children while I was at work. He was very involved."

Eve (Council): "For my second child my husband changed jobs so we managed to arrange childcare between us. He gave up a full-time job and went to work part time for [supermarket]. I used to work Mondays, Tuesdays and Wednesdays and he would work Thursdays, Fridays and Saturdays. Since then he's working more full-time hours."

---

[14] La Valle et al's study (2002) also identified the category of 'shift parenting' where "the working hours of each partner are organised in a way that between them they can be available to look after the children". As in this study, 'shift parenting' was found in families with children under the age of 10. Most parents included in our 'shift parenting' category shared responsibilities more or less equally, and some of our 'joint female biased' examples of parenting would be included in La Valle et al's 'shift parenting' category.

Jeremy (Shopwell): "I used to work on the railways and so it was one day on and one day off and so we shared childcare ourselves up until the children were seven and five. We both worked on the railways and so we could manage our shifts quite well. Childcare now is fairly equally shared between us. I fit my rota around what she's working."

Many instances of shift parenting involved the combination of two relatively low-level (and low-paid) jobs. Thus shift parenting often, but not always, has a class dimension. However, in some cases of shift parenting fathers/husbands had remained in a lower-level occupation so as to be able to give their wives domestic support while they gained qualifications and developed their careers, as in the case of Joyce. Joyce's husband, who has a low-level job, had actively encouraged her to gain professional qualifications, and she describes their current childcare arrangements as follows:

Joyce (Council): "We share. He works nights. I don't get home from work until half four, quarter to five, so we all sit down to a meal together. So he cooks meals during the week. At weekends I tend to do more with the younger one because I haven't seen so much of her during the week. Sundays we try and make a family day."

In a few cases, fathers did most of the childcare. Kerry's husband is the main carer of their children:

Kerry (Cellbank): "My husband looks after them. I normally drop them off at school and get in at half nine, then I work until later on in the evening. My husband picks them up from school. In the holidays I try to take as much of my holiday in the school holidays as possible, and then my husband has them the rest of the time. [When they were young] he did full-time childcare."

Other fathers had also taken on major childcare responsibilities, but usually this was *involuntary*, that is, they had lost their jobs and/or been made redundant.

Philip (Cellbank): "Unfortunately I was made redundant around the time my oldest was three, so I looked after him for about six months until I found full-time employment."

During these periods, some men had cared for their children while their wives worked or studied:

Frank (Shopwell): "It just so happened that my redundancy coincided with her starting out as a student. Our roles changed. On and off over the past five years I've been unemployed and employed, so the times I was unemployed I was looking after my son. I would take him to school. All sorts of things. And doing that as well as the household chores. So the roles changed about five years ago."

Frank, like Joyce's husband, had provided domestic support for his wife while she trained for a professional occupation, and as he put it: "my role, without being sexist, is like that of the lady of the house". However, only one of the men interviewed had *voluntarily* changed their hours of work in order to look after their children. Again, Charles had supported his wife's career development:

Charles (Council): "... my wife was in full-time education and she wasn't bringing in much money, and I was out a lot as well, and what with the new baby. That was very difficult, managing the time thing. After about a year of trying to cope with that, that's when I decided to change and come here. When I first started it was only three days a week, which was perfect, although our income dropped again. But I was able to do three days here a week and have two days at home – four days including the weekends – and could share the responsibilities with the children, and it enabled my wife to continue with her study and catch up on those two days."

Employed parents, therefore, use a variety of arrangements in combining work and childcare. Probably the most common is a modified version of the male breadwinner model, either *female dominant* or *joint female biased* parenting. A substantial minority of parents of younger children, however, share childcare and in many cases of *shift parenting*, childcare was more or less equally balanced between partners.

We should emphasise that the categories of parenting arrangements that we have identified are for illustrative purposes only, and should not be taken as fixed. *Male biased* parenting would seem to be largely a consequence of economic pressures and therefore likely to be relatively unstable; *female biased* parenting is likely to be a more stable arrangement.

Non-parental childcare

We have focused mainly on the parental division of labour in respect of childcare, but of course most working parents also use other forms of childcare as well. As is well known, grandparents are the most important source of childcare assistance (Finlayson et al, 1996), and this was also the case among the parents we interviewed. Interviewees in Sheffield were more likely to be able to call on grandparental help than interviewees in East/Kent Canterbury. As described in Yeandle et al (2002), the level of geographical mobility is much higher in East Kent/Canterbury than in Sheffield, thus assistance from kin is more likely to be available in Sheffield[15].

Nevertheless, in both localities grandparents were an important resource, and indeed, were often involved in 'shift parenting':

Charlotte (Shopwell): "It's mainly been my mum since I've worked. We coordinate our shifts because we both work at Shopwell. But I suppose our shifts coincided quite a bit so we didn't really have to change the shifts much."

In some cases grandparents were the sole providers of non-parental care:

Emma (Cellbank): "Luckily enough for me we have both sets of parents living close by. So my husband's mum looks after them four out of the five days, and my mum does two afternoons.... I did use nursery in as much as I wanted them to socialise with other children. [And what about school holidays? How do you manage?] My mother-in-law does all of them."

[15] In fact, 21 of our East Kent/Canterbury interviewees had been geographically mobile, as compared to only three of the Sheffield interviewees.

Shauna (Council): "Her grandparents have looked after her. My parents and in-laws."

More often, however, parents of younger children drew on a variety of sources for childcare:

Ursula (Council): "In the early years I used a childminder, then both childminder and nursery. At one time I had a nanny (not a live in one). As they each started school I used the school after-school club. Now they are both at school, one junior, one senior. I also have very supportive parents who help out whenever needed."

Beth (Cellbank): "I have used a childminder, nursery, grandparents, a mixture of all three at the same time."

As with parental childcare arrangements, therefore, non-parental childcare strategies are extremely fluid. Although it might be useful to think of a 'kin care to private (paid) care' continuum, therefore, it is of equal importance to emphasise that care arrangements will change and develop during the period of the child's dependency.

Concluding discussion: men's attitudes to work–life balance

In this chapter, we have examined how men and women thought about their individual careers and the (often conflicting) demands of family life, as well as the diverse ways in which families organised their employment and family lives. In general, attitudes to family life and gender roles in Britain have changed considerably over the last 50 years. Children are no longer seen and not heard, and in marriage ceremonies, wives no longer routinely promise to 'obey' their husbands.

How men (and women) divide up responsibilities for breadwinning and caring work will be an outcome of both their own ideas and motivations as well as the particular set of circumstances in which they find themselves. As we have seen, a small minority of fathers had at some time or other assumed a substantial responsibility for childcare. In most of these cases, however, it was transformations in their

working lives (that is, a period of unemployment) that had brought about changes in their family arrangements. These cases indicate that despite the very real changes that have taken place in gender relations and family lives, the characteristic direction of the structuring of the employment/family relationship for men and women remains broadly unchanged. That is, for women, changes in family circumstances are likely to lead to changes in their employment, whereas for men, changes in their employment circumstances had led to changes in their family arrangements.

Nevertheless, among our interviewees, a number of men had, either by accident or design, positively encouraged the career development of their partners by taking on an enhanced domestic role. Although, therefore, in most households the man will be the major earner and parenting responsibilities will be biased towards the mother, the continuing growth of women's aspirations and qualification levels is likely to contribute to a gradual increase in joint and/or father-biased parenting.

However, recent research carried out in Norway (Brandth and Kvande, 2002) suggests that motivation among men (and women) remains very important. In Norway, recent reforms have introduced a mandatory quota of four weeks' parental leave, to be forfeited if not taken up (that is, not transferable to the mother). Other provisions include 14 'daddy days' at the birth of a child, and a time account scheme that includes flexible leave arrangements and the right to work part time. The use by fathers of this six weeks' entitlement varied according to employment circumstances. The full six weeks was more likely to be taken up in the public sector than in the private sector, and by fathers with higher levels of education. Fathers who were self-employed, those who worked a lot of overtime and those in senior managerial positions, were less likely to take the six weeks. Thus structural constraints remain significant. At the individual level, however, there were fathers in demanding jobs and careers who took the full six weeks (and more unpaid leave under the time account scheme) despite considerable pressures from their employers: they were strongly motivated to stay at home. Other fathers with high-flying careers took the minimum leave: they gave their jobs priority. Other fathers took the full six weeks but (being low paid) could not consider taking unpaid leave in addition because of the potential loss of income to the family.

Our evidence suggests a similar mixture of choice and constraint among the men we interviewed. Some fathers were highly family-oriented and indeed argued that work–life policies should be extended.

> Scott (Cellbank): "I don't think that five carers' days in a year is enough. If you've got someone who needs long-term care, it's not going to go very far. If you've got a child who's ill, they're going to be sick more than five times in a year, aren't they. So I think we're making noises but we're not there yet. It's very difficult. A company doesn't employ you to care for your parents, does it? They employ you to work, looking at it from the business point of view."

Charles (Council) had taken a drop in income in order to be able to make a greater contribution to childcare. Other men had not been involved in childcare:

> Eric (Cellbank): "My wife didn't work until the children were at school. Then she took jobs that would allow her to get to school, pick them up from school and have holidays off. Dinner lady, working at home, that sort of work."

Nevertheless, in general, men were aware of the need to recognise and appreciate caring responsibilities within the employment context. As one of our older interviewees robustly put it:

> Fred (Council): "I would think that if they did have a disabled wife or whatever, generally speaking, anybody would allow a bit of leeway. They would have to be a double toerag [not to]."

In summary, among the majority of our interviewees, women had taken the greater responsibility for childcare, often to the detriment of their careers. They may have 'chosen' to do so, but often, this 'choice' was structured by lack of alternatives. Among interviewees with younger children, most women still took the major responsibility for childcare but many fathers were also much involved, particularly in cases of 'shift parenting'. Both men and women recognised that caring responsibilities made it difficult to pursue a career, but more women than men had not pursued a career for family reasons. Some men, however, had actively encouraged the career development of their partners by taking on an enhanced domestic role.

In general, both men and women were sensitive to family-friendly issues and it did not seem that men considered family 'claims' to be any less legitimate than women did although, of course, there were individual variations among both sexes. But, as Harry (Council) put it, "As far as I'm concerned family should always come first".

Conclusions

5

In this report, we have examined some of the parallel changes in employment, family life and women's behaviour and aspirations that have been underway over the last few decades. Relationships both within families and employment have become more flexible. As the 'male breadwinner' model of employment and family life changes, do parallel changes in the workplace make it more or less difficult to combine paid employment and employment careers with caring responsibilities of all kinds? Our research objectives included exploring the impact of flexible working and employment breaks on individual careers for men and women, assessing the impact of organisational culture on the take-up and impact of family-friendly policies, and exploring men's attitudes to family-friendly working arrangements.

Most of the men who had taken an employment break had done so involuntarily. Charles, who had taken a part-time job in order to share childcare with his wife, had 'downshifted' with the advent of family responsibilities, and his career had not progressed as far as it would have done otherwise – but it is problematic to generalise from a 'sample' of one. More generally, in respect of the impact of flexible working and employment breaks on individual employment careers, there were sharp differences between the three organisations studied. Both Cellbank and Shopwell had recently shifted to individualised career paths and the onus was now on the individual, rather than the organisation, to develop their career. However, in Cellbank the long service of most employees meant that the impact of the past strategy of classic bureaucratic administration, when full-time work and unbroken service was expected of 'career' employees, was still very evident. Thus, in general, employees who had

taken career breaks or switched to part-time working (and these were all women) had not progressed as far up the career ladder as those who had not done so.

Our evidence, however, also showed that improvements had been made, and career-oriented women returners can now be offered part-time work at higher-grade levels. Nevertheless, both men and women in Cellbank recognised that taking on even a lower-level managerial position would mean longer working hours. Furthermore, although higher-level part-time jobs were available in Cellbank, many managerial women (for example, Peggy and Abigail) considered that full-time work was necessary in order to demonstrate full career commitment.

In Shopwell, the relatively low level of formal qualifications among employees means that only a minority would ever have anticipated an employment 'career' in the conventional or stereotypical sense (some Shopwell employees, however, had been displaced from orthodox employment careers into work at Shopwell). The heterogeneous employment background of the majority of Shopwell employees means that employment breaks as such are not a particular disadvantage as far as careers in Shopwell are concerned and, indeed, many Shopwell employees are relatively short-service workers in any case. At the basic employee level, employment at Shopwell is extremely flexible and good policies are available (but key aspects of these policies, such as shift swaps and long holiday leave, are unpaid). However, Shopwell managers work full time. Given that a large part of their job is to ensure that cover is provided within their departments/area of responsibility, managers at Shopwell work long hours, and this would seem to be widely expected. Their jobs, therefore, are not particularly family friendly.

The situation in the Councils was more mixed than in Shopwell or Cellbank. In general, breaks in employment, and shifts to part-time work, had had a negative impact on the development of individual career paths and, as in Cellbank, the bureaucratic past still strongly marks the present (and has in any case been less radically changed). However, in the Councils there were more jobs available (in comparison to Shopwell and Cellbank) where the particular skills, or professional qualification, of the individual concerned were the primary prerequisites for the job itself. As with other highly skilled and qualified individuals (such as teachers, doctors, accountants, pharmacists, IT specialists, and so on), it is possible to work flexibly in these occupations without slipping to lower grades, and to take career breaks without suffering occupational downgrading[16].

What this study of three very different types of organisation has revealed, therefore, is patterns of both continuity and change. Organisations have changed, and flexible job opportunities are increasingly available. Nevertheless, what has not changed is that in all four organisations studied, higher-level 'career' jobs usually entailed full-time work (and often, long hours). The people working for organisations have changed as well, particularly women, who are increasingly concerned with career development. What has not changed, however, is that most women still take the major responsibility for home and childcare. It is widely recognised that career development will require full-time working (and possibly longer hours), thus many women (and some men) 'choose' to rein back their career development in favour of family life (Becker and Moen, 1999).

Thus, both particular kinds of employment, and the skills and qualifications of particular kinds of

employee, have different outcomes as far as the capacity to achieve work–life integration is concerned. A similar argument as to the significance of occupational variations for work–life balance has been made in a review and summary of recent research findings:

> Any ... approach ... cannot ignore the intractable phenomenon of occupational class.... Women in managerial and professional jobs with higher incomes and benefits are in a much better position to achieve a (work–life) balance than their much lower-paid and insecure counterparts employed, for example, in the retail trade and textiles. (Taylor, 2001, p 18)

However, although we would agree with the general argument as to the significance of occupational variations, our findings suggest that the argument quoted above should be modified. In our research, low-paid workers in retail, in relatively undemanding jobs, were among those finding it the most possible to achieve the practicalities of work–life balance. However, since these jobs were low-paid, in some cases an explicit trade-off was being made between income and employment flexibility. Indeed, as Blossfeld and Drobnic have argued, "the decrease in gender inequality in terms of labour-force participation is accompanied by an increase in social class inequalities" (2001, p 381).

Work–life 'balance' (or articulation) has an experiential, as well as a practical, dimension. That is, families with employed parents/carers may experience more or less stress. Families in which women (and men) take up low-paid, flexible employment in order to achieve the practicalities of work–life balance may experience less stress, but, as we have emphasised, at some material cost. As we have seen, it was widely understood among our interviewees that more demanding (and better paid) jobs will require longer hours and, in the case of line managerial jobs, will be less flexible. Thus, as has been demonstrated in a recent survey, individuals in managerial jobs express a higher level of work–life stress (Crompton et al, 2003).

Occupational class categories describe not only the incomes and benefits attached to particular occupations, but also the wider employment and career opportunities associated with the category

---

[16] Individuals with specific skills and/or professional qualifications who wish to develop a 'professional career' – that is, to achieve higher-level positions within their own occupations (for example, principal officer in a local authority finance department, or a headteacher in a school) – will have to work full time. The point being made here is that specific occupational skills offer protection from occupational downgrading such as (for example) experienced by Alice (Chapter 2).

– that is, 'life chances'. Individual skills and qualifications, as well as occupational/ organisational assets (see the discussion in Chapter 2), together contribute to the 'life chances' of those in employment. In some occupations (in particular, professions such as law and medicine), individual skills and qualifications are key requirements for entry to the occupation. This has implications for work–life balance, in that well-qualified professionals can choose family-friendly, flexible employment careers.

However, people without specific qualifications and/or those who are relatively unqualified who want to work their way up to managerial positions in organisations such as Shopwell and Cellbank will face 'long hours' working. Although, perhaps, employment breaks as such are becoming less important to individual career development, getting qualifications early on is becoming more important if individuals want to achieve flexible working at reasonable rates of pay. In respect of the capacity to 'choose' to work flexibly, therefore, we would draw a distinction between professional and managerial employment. As other research has demonstrated, individuals with externally validated skills and qualifications – such as, for example, teachers, accountants, lawyers, health or environmental specialists – are enabled, if they wish, to find employment (for example, part-time or short-term work) that meshes with their other priorities and responsibilities, including caring responsibilities (Crompton, 1999, 2001). Such individuals will not necessarily maximise their economic returns, but the professional 'rate for the job' will ensure a reasonable level of income.

In all three of the organisations we studied, managers usually worked longer hours than contracted. Full-time employment, and a willingness to work long hours, was seen as a measure of commitment in career terms. Thus, although a career break (or more usually, a period of part-time working) might be compatible with subsequent career development, part-time workers are not seen to be 'careerists' and moreover, often do not see themselves as such. National surveys suggest an increase in work intensity in the UK over the last decade (Taylor, 2001; Burchell et al, 2002), and indeed, it is often suggested that Britain has a 'long hours culture'. Although we would not necessarily disagree with this broad assertion, we would

suggest that the notion of 'culture' needs to be unpacked. Do people feel they *ought* to work long hours (in a moral sense), do people *need* to work the hours in order to make up their pay, and/or do people *have* to work longer hours than they would like to because of the pressures of work? 'Long hours culture' is a problematic term, and we should be wary of blanket generalisations.

It might be argued that those who work long hours to build a career have 'chosen' to do so. In this sense, a 'long hours culture' reflects an internalised commitment. Some people need to work long hours because of financial reasons, but this cannot be described as a culture in the sense of an individual's belief in the desirability of the situation. But also, as we have seen, policies of 'lean' staffing makes taking time off – even if work–life policies are available – very difficult. This can hardly be described as a 'culture', and is more a consequence of work intensification. Most people interviewed felt entitled to take advantage of the work–life policies available, but many felt they would let their work colleagues down if they were absent (particularly in Cellbank and the Councils). It is paradoxical, therefore, that despite the fact that new managerial techniques promote a culture of individualisation, in these instances it is a feeling of solidarity with colleagues that sustains organisational functioning[17]. Indeed, in the case of Cellbank we found that different aspects of organisational policies and culture were pulling in different directions. Cellbank wished to promote family-friendliness as part of its policy to become the 'employer of choice', but policies of target setting (for example, in respect of credit card sales) and lean staffing made the implementation of family-friendly policies problematic.

Our analysis included men as well as women. Among the men and women we interviewed, we did not find markedly different attitudes towards work/family balance. In general most said that they would put their families first. However, far

---

[17] It is often argued that smaller firms and organisations will be disadvantaged if family-friendly policies are instituted as a right (DTI, 2000; Taylor, 2001). While it is the case that smaller organisations will be relatively more affected by the absence of an employee, our evidence suggests that it is the size of the unit, rather than the size of the firm as such, that is crucial.

more women than men had curtailed their career aspirations and development on account of their families. In terms of the distribution of parenting and paid work, substantial changes had taken place among parents of children under the age of 10, in that a much higher proportion of these mothers had remained in paid work (often part-time work) while their children were under school age than mothers of older children. Many of these women took the major responsibility for childcare, but this should not detract from the fact that many men were also reported as taking a major role in childcare, particularly in cases of 'shift parenting'. Many cases of 'shift parenting' involved partners who each had a low-paid job, reflecting the fact that many lower-level jobs, even when they are full time, do not provide sufficient income to adequately support a household.

Shift parenting, therefore, has a class dimension but it is not only found in low-income households. In some cases the partners of women who had been occupationally successful had taken on flexible, but full-time, employment that fitted around their wives' work patterns. Some men had taken on enhanced domestic responsibilities so that their wives could undertake professional training and develop their careers. There were also instances of partners, both in full-time jobs, in which family responsibilities were shared. In a number of families, therefore, the balance of employment and unpaid caring between men and women is changing, but men who take on a larger share of caring responsibilities tend not to give up employment, but to work full time in a lower-level job, and/or forgo or put limits on their own career opportunities.

In summary, our research findings reflect both continuity and change. New developments in workplace organisation and administration, often using sophisticated computer applications, have made it increasingly more possible to offer flexible employment solutions that enhance the possibilities of balancing work and family life[18]. However, some of these flexible jobs, as in the case of Shopwell, will not generate sufficient income to support a family, even given a full-time working week. Employers and policy makers have become increasingly aware of the caring responsibilities of their employees. What

has not changed, however, is the fact that promotion to a managerial position entails full-time working and, as a general rule, a willingness to work longer hours than contracted. Among our respondents, combining an upwardly mobile employment career with extensive family responsibilities was widely seen as problematic. Employers may have good intentions, but nevertheless, they also have to achieve their business and organisational objectives.

Thus, as other empirical research (for example, Hochschild, 1997) has consistently demonstrated, there will be a continuing tension between business imperatives and requirements for caring (of all kinds) that is not amenable to any easy resolution. This does not mean that the search for possible solutions should be abandoned. Employee productivity might not necessarily be enhanced by lean staffing and work intensification, factors that may be associated with low staff morale and excessive labour turnover. It may be more productive to reorganise work with a view to reducing employee stress – and work–life imbalance may be highly stressful – rather than minimising the number of employees per se. However, answers will also have to be found in the development of more systematic public policies directed towards these issues, as a number of recent commentators have argued (Taylor, 2001; Burchell et al, 2002).

Finally, we have also identified continuity and change in both the relationships and divisions of labour between men and women. Among our interviewees, in the majority of cases women still take the major responsibility for unpaid caring work and are also considerably more likely to curb their career aspirations because of caring responsibilities. Nevertheless, some women (with caring responsibilities) have well-articulated employment career plans. However, and particularly among younger parents, men are taking on a greater share of caring responsibilities although, unlike past generations of women, such men do not usually give up full-time work. In conclusion, therefore, it may be anticipated that these changes in gender relations will bring about greater pressures from women *and men* for the introduction of policies to achieve work–life integration.

---

[18] See, for example, www.timecare.com

References

Arthur, M. and Rousseau, D. (eds) (1996) *The boundaryless career: A new employment principle for a new organisational era*, Oxford: Oxford University Press.

Becker, P.E. and Moen, P. (1999) 'Scaling back: dual-earner couples' work–family strategies', *Journal of Marriage and the Family*, vol 61, pp 995-1007.

Blossfeld, H.-P. and Drobnic, S. (eds) (2001) *Careers of couples in contemporary society: From male breadwinner to dual-earner families*, Oxford: Oxford University Press.

Brandth, B. and Kvande, E. (2002) 'Reflexive fathers: negotiating parental leave and working life', *Gender, Work and Organization*, vol 9, no 2, pp 186-203.

Burchell, B., Ladipo, D. and Wilkinson, F. (eds) (2002) *Job insecurity and work intensification*, London and New York, NY: Routledge.

Butler, T. and Savage, M. (eds) (1996) *Social change and the middle classes*, London: UCL Press.

Cockburn, C. (1991) *In the way of women*, Basingstoke: Macmillan.

Crompton, R. (1986) 'Women and the "service class"', in R. Crompton and M. Mann (eds) *Gender and stratification*, Cambridge: Polity, pp 117-36.

Crompton, R. (1989) 'Women in banking', *Work, Employment and Society*, vol 3, no 2, pp 141-56.

Crompton, R. (1997) *Women and work in modern Britain*, Oxford: Oxford University Press.

Crompton, R. (ed) (1999) *Restructuring gender relations and employment*, Oxford: Oxford University Press.

Crompton, R. (2001) 'Gender restructuring, employment, and caring', *Social Politics*, Fall, pp 266-91.

Crompton, R. and Harris, F. (1998) 'Gender relations and employment: the impact of occupation', *Work, Employment and Society*, vol 12, no 2, pp 297-315.

Crompton, R., Brockmann, M. and Wiggins, R. (2003) 'Women's employment, gender roles and work–life balance', *British Social Attitudes': 20th Report*, London: Sage Publications.

Davidson, M. and Cooper, C. (1992) *Shattering the glass ceiling*, London: Paul Chapman Publishing.

Dench, S., Aston, L., Evans, C., Meager, N., Williams, M. and Willison, R. (2002) *Key indicators of women's position in Britain*, London: DTI Publishing.

Dex, S. (1987) *Women's occupational mobility*, Basingstoke: Macmillan.

Dex, S. and McCulloch, A. (1997) *Flexible employment*, Houndmills and London: Macmillan.

Dex, S. and Smith, C. (2002) *The nature and pattern of family-friendly employment policies in Britain*, Bristol/York: The Policy Press/ Joseph Rowntree Foundation.

DTI (Department for Trade and Industry) (2000) *Work and parents: Competitiveness and choice*, London: The Stationery Office.

DTI/HM Treasury (2003) *Balancing work and family life: Enhancing choice and support for parents*, London: The Stationery Office.

du Gay, P. (1996) *Consumption and identity at work*, London: Sage Publications.

Fagan, C. (2001) 'Time, money and the gender order: work orientations and working-time preferences in Britain', *Gender Work and Organization*, vol 8, no 3, pp 239-66.

Finch, J. (1983) *Married to the job*, London: George Allen and Unwin.

Finlayson, L., Ford, R. and Marsh, A. (1996) 'Paying more for child care', *Employment Gazette*, July, pp 295-303.

Forth, J., Lissenburgh, S., Callender, C. and Millward, N. (1997) *Family-friendly working arrangements in Britain*, Research Report No 16, London: DfEE.

Green, A.E. and Canny, A. (2003) *Geographical mobility: Family impacts*, Bristol/York: The Policy Press/Joseph Rowntree Foundation.

Grimshaw, D., Beynon, H., Rubery, J. and Ward, K. (2002) 'The restructuring of career paths in large service sector organisations: "delayering", upskilling and polarisation', *Sociological Review*, vol 3, pp 89-115.

Grimshaw, D., Ward, K., Rubery, J. and Beynon, H. (2001) 'Organisations and the transformation of the internal labour market in the UK', *Work, Employment and Society*, vol 15, no 1, pp 25-54.

Grint, K. (1991) *The sociology of work*, Cambridge: Polity.

Hakim, C. (1979) *Occupational segregation*, Research Paper No 9, London: Department of Employment.

Hakim, C. (2000) *Work–lifestyle choices in the 21st century: Preference theory*, Oxford: Oxford University Press.

Halford, S., Savage, M. and Witz, A. (1997) *Gender, careers and organisations*, Basingstoke: Macmillan.

Handy, C. (1994) *The empty raincoat*, London: Hutchinson.

Hochschild, A. (1997) *The time bind*, New York, NY: Metropolitan Books.

Hojgaard, L. (1997) 'Working fathers: caught in the web of the symbolic order of gender', *Acta Sociologica*, vol 40, pp 245-61.

Hojgaard, L. (1998) 'Family-supportive policies in the workplace', in E. Drew, R. Emerek and E. Mahon (eds) *Women, work and the family in Europe*, London: Routledge, pp 140-9.

Kanter, R. (1977) *Men and women of the corporation*, New York, NY: Basic Books.

La Valle, I., Arthur, S., Millward, C., Scott, J. with Clayden, M. (2002) *Happy families? Atypical work and its influence on family life*, Bristol/York: The Policy Press/Joseph Rowntree Foundation.

Lewis, S. (1997) 'Family-friendly employment policies: a route to changing organisational culture or playing about at the margins?', *Gender, Work and Organisation*, vol 4, no 1, pp 1-23.

McGovern, P., Hope-Hailey, V. and Stiles, P. (1998) 'The managerial career after downsizing', *Work, Employment and Society*, vol 12, no 3, pp 457-77.

McRae, S, (1996) *Maternity rights in Britain*, London: Policy Studies Institute.

Peters, T. and Waterman, R. (1982) *In search of excellence*, New York, NY: Harper and Row.

Phillips, J., Bernard, M. and Chittenden, M. (2002) *Juggling work and care: The experiences of working carers of older adults*, Bristol/York: The Policy Press/Joseph Rowntree Foundation.

Purcell, K., Hogarth, T. and Simm, C. (1999) *Whose flexibility?*, York: Joseph Rowntree Foundation.

Rose, N. (1993) 'Government, authority and expertise in advanced liberalism', *Economy and Society*, vol 22, no 3, pp 283-99.

Savage, M., Dickens, A. and Fielding, T. (1992) *Property, bureaucracy and culture: Middle class formation in contemporary Britain*, London: Routledge.

Sennett, R. (1998) *The corrosion of character*, New York, NY and London: W.W. Norton and Company.

Taylor, R. (2001) *The future of work–life balance*, Swindon: Economic and Social Research Council.

Thompson, P. and Warhurst, C. (ed) (1998) *Workplaces of the future*, Basingstoke: Macmillan.

Wacjman, J. (1998) *Managing like a man*, Cambridge: Polity.

Wacjman, J. and Martin, B. (2001) 'My company or my career: managerial achievement and loyalty', *British Journal of Sociology*, vol 52, no 4, 559-78.

Womack, J., Jones, D. and Roos, D. (1990) *The machine that changed the world*, New York, NY: Macmillan.

Yeandle, S., Wigfield, A., Crompton, R. and Dennett, J. (2002) *Employed carers and family-friendly employment policies*, Bristol/York: The Policy Press/Joseph Rowntree Foundation.

Appendix A: Interview schedule

Organisations, careers and caring

What is your job title?

Are you married/do you have a partner living with you?

Does your partner go out to work? If yes, what job do they do?

Do you have any children? If yes, how many and how old are they?

How do you/did you manage childcare?

How far would you say your partner was involved? What about sharing childcare? Who does what?

Do you have any other caring* responsibilities (parents, spouse/partner, other relative, friend)? Have you been a carer in the past?

If yes, can you tell me more about it? Who do or did you care for? How do you or did you manage? Do the people you care for have any other help?

If no, do you think you might ever have to provide care for someone?

What is your highest educational qualification?

What is/was your father's main paid job?

What is/was your mother's main paid job?

Going back to your schooldays, can you remember if you had any ideas or ambitions about what you wanted to do when you left school? *Any particular occupation or career, travel, marriage and family, anything else?*

Was there anyone who particularly encouraged you when you were younger? *Teacher, family member, friend, anyone else?*

Did they encourage you to do anything in particular?

When you were thinking about what job to do, did you ever think about how it might fit in with your family and domestic life?

What year were you born?

Going back over your adult life – can I just go through with you the kinds of things you've done? (*Fill in a lifeline for each interviewee.*)

Do you think of yourself as a 'career' person? *Probe on careers within the organisation.*

If has taken maternity leave: do you think this had any impact on how you were seen at work? How did you feel about this?

If hasn't taken maternity leave: do you think it's difficult for women to get back into work after maternity leave?

If has taken employment breaks: how did you feel about this at the time?

If hasn't taken employment breaks: do people ever take employment breaks? How does it work out?

If has taken employment breaks: did you ever consider not taking these breaks?

If hasn't taken breaks: would you ever consider taking a break?

If has taken employment breaks: has taking a break caused any problems as far as work was concerned? How did you feel about going back?

If hasn't: have you ever considered taking a break from work? If so, why didn't you take a career break in the end? Do you think it would make a difference to your career prospects if you did?

Are you happy with the way your career (working life) has gone so far?

---

* 'Caring' means that you are in some way responsible for another person. This might include day-to-day care, as in the case of young children or a disabled person, but it could also include collecting a child from school, doing the shopping or collecting a prescription for an older person, or simply visiting someone regularly to check on their welfare.

Would you like to go further? Are there good career prospects within the organisation? What are they?

And how about the family/domestic side of things – are you happy with the way things have gone?

How long have you been with your current employer?

How many hours a week do you usually work? Is that how many you are contracted to work?

In general, do you think people work longer hours nowadays? Why do you think this is?

Would you call the organisation you work for 'family friendly'? By 'family-friendly' policies we mean how easy does your employer make it for people to balance their work and family responsibilities?

And what about your workmates – how do they react to people who have childcare responsibilities or are caring for older or disabled people? Do you think enough or too much is done to accommodate people with caring responsibilities?

For carers: how have your managers (past and present) reacted to your caring responsibilities? *Probe on problems with time.* Do other managers react the same way?

For non-carers: how do your managers tend to treat people with caring responsibilities? Do other managers behave the same way? *Probe on problems with cover.*

For carers: how do you feel about taking time off for family or domestic reasons? *Do you ever feel guilty re colleagues, management?*

For non-carers: how do you feel about other people taking time off for family or domestic reasons?

As far as your present workplace is concerned – would you have any suggestions for how things might be improved?

Roughly, what is your annual *household* income?
- ☐ Less than £15,000
- ☐ £15,001-£20,000
- ☐ £20,001-£30,000
- ☐ £30,001-£40,000
- ☐ £40,001-£50,000
- ☐ More than £50,000
- ☐ Prefer not to say

Looking back over the things we've talked about, are there any things you would like to add? Do you think we have left anything out?

Thank you very much (*and reassure of confidentiality*).

May we contact you again? *If so, check that the contact details are correct.*

Appendix B:
All interviews (listed in alphabetical order of pseudonym)

Ref	Pseudonym	Sex	Age	Location	Sector	Grade	Qualifications	Children	Age of youngest child	Other caring	Annual household income	Contracted hours	Actual hours	Career path[a]
9	Abigail	F	30	Canterbury	Cellbank	G3	A level or equivalent	yes	10 or under	no	£40,001-£50,000	PT	<5 extra hrs no extra pay	no break, change hours
1	Adam	M	29	Canterbury	Cellbank	G4+	A level or equivalent	no		no	£40,001-£50,000	FT	<5 extra hrs no extra pay	no break
99	Agatha	F	43	Sheffield	Council	G10+	Postgrad qualification	no		yes	More than £50,000	FT	<15 extra hrs no extra pay	no break
28	Alec	M	43	Canterbury	Council	G6-9	GCSE or equivalent	yes	11-16	no	£40,001-£50,000	FT	<15 extra hrs no extra pay	no break
57	Alice	F	35	Canterbury	Shopwell	Shopfloor	A level or equivalent	yes	10 or under	no	£15,001-£20,000	PT	contracted	no break, change hours
23	Alison	F	57	Canterbury	Cellbank	G1	A level or equivalent	yes	17+	no	£20,001-£30,000	PT	contracted	break
90	Anthony	M	38	Sheffield	Council	G6-9	A level or equivalent	yes	10 or under	no	£30,001-£40,000	FT	contracted	no break
126	Audrey	F	57	Sheffield	Shopwell	Shopfloor	Commercial qualifications	yes	17+	no	Can't/prefer not to say	FT	contracted	break
56	Barbara	F	34	Canterbury	Shopwell	Shopfloor	GCSE or equivalent	yes	11-16	no	Can't/prefer not to say	FT	extra for overtime	break
112	Barry	M	52	Sheffield	Shopwell	Manager	No qualifications	yes	10 or under	no	£30,001-£40,000	FT	many more, no extra pay	no break
83	Beth	F	39	Sheffield	Cellbank	G3	A level or equivalent	yes	10 or under	no	£40,001-£50,000	FT	flexi, no problems	no break, change hours
2	Bill	M	33	Canterbury	Cellbank	G3	A level or equivalent	yes	10 or under	no	£20,001-£30,000	FT	contracted	no break
55	Carolyn	F	27	Canterbury	Shopwell	Shopfloor	GCSE or equivalent	no		no	Can't/prefer not to say	FT	contracted	no break
78	Cassie	F	31	Sheffield	Cellbank	G1	A level or equivalent	yes	10 or under	no	£20,001-£30,000	PT	extra for overtime	no break, change hours
124	Celia	F	53	Sheffield	Shopwell	Shopfloor	GCSE or equivalent	yes	17+	yes	£15,001-£20,000	PT	extra for overtime	break

Ref	Pseudonym	Sex	Age	Location	Sector	Grade	Qualifications	Children	Age of youngest child	Other caring	Annual household income	Contracted hours	Actual hours	Career path[a]
27	Charles	M	39	Canterbury	Council	G6-9	Higher education below degree	yes	10 or under	no	£40,001–£50,000	FT	<15 extra hrs no extra pay	break
114	Charlotte	F	34	Sheffield	Shopwell	Shopfloor	GCSE or equivalent	yes	10 or under	no	£15,001–£20,000	PT	contracted	no break, change hours
117	Chloe	F	38	Sheffield	Shopwell	Shopfloor	GCSE or equivalent	yes	11–16	no	£15,001–£20,000	FT	contracted	break
70	Cliff	M	39	Sheffield	Cellbank	G4+	ACIB	yes	10 or under	no	£20,001–£30,000	FT	<15 extra hrs no extra pay	no break
50	Craig	M	40	Canterbury	Shopwell	Manager	A level or equivalent	yes	11–16	no	More than £50,000	FT	<15 extra hrs no extra pay	no break
54	Cyril	M	63	Canterbury	Shopwell	Shopfloor	No qualifications	yes	17+	yes	Less than £15,000	FT	extra for overtime	no break
12	Daisy	F	38	Canterbury	Cellbank	G3	GCSE or equivalent	yes	10 or under	no	More than £50,000	PT	contracted	break
108	Daniel	M	34	Sheffield	Shopwell	Manager	GCSE or equivalent	yes	10 or under	no	More than £50,000	FT	<5 extra hrs no extra pay	no break
22	Daphne	F	55	Canterbury	Cellbank	G1	Commercial qualifications	yes	17+	no	Can't/prefer not to say	FT	<5 extra hrs no extra pay	break
49	Darius	M	37	Canterbury	Shopwell	Shopfloor		yes	10 or under	yes	Less than £15,000	FT	extra for overtime	no break
60	Debbie	F	44	Canterbury	Shopwell	Shopfloor	No qualifications	yes	11–16	yes	Can't/prefer not to say	FT	extra for overtime	no break, change hours
6	Dennis	M	44	Canterbury	Cellbank	G4+	ACIB	yes	10 or under	no	£30,001–£40,000	FT	contracted	no break
30	Derek	M	52	Canterbury	Council	G10+	Degree or equivalent	yes	11–16	yes	£30,001–£40,000	FT	<5 extra hrs no extra pay	no break
52	Donald	M	59	Canterbury	Shopwell	Manager	No qualifications	yes	17+	yes	£15,001–£20,000	FT	many more, no extra pay	no break
113	Donna	F	30	Sheffield	Shopwell	Shopfloor	Apprentice	yes	10 or under	yes	£20,001–£30,000	PT	occ more no extra pay	no break, change hours

Ref	Pseudonym	Sex	Age	Location	Sector	Grade	Qualifications	Children	Age of youngest child	Other caring	Annual household income	Contracted hours	Actual hours	Career path[a]
103	Dulcie	F	51	Sheffield	Council	G1	GCSE or equivalent	yes	17+	no	£20,001–£30,000	FT	contracted	break
29	Ed	M	50	Canterbury	Council	G6-9	A level or equivalent	yes	17+	no	£20,001–£30,000	FT	contracted	no break
86	Elaine	F	47	Sheffield	Cellbank	G2	No qualifications	no		yes	£15,001–£20,000	FT	occ more no extra pay	no break
59	Elena	F	41	Canterbury	Shopwell	Shopfloor	GCSE or equivalent	yes	11–16	no	Less than £15,000	PT	extra for overtime	break
106	Elsie	F	61	Sheffield	Council	G6-9	Postgrad qualification	yes	17+	no	£30,001–£40,000	FT	contracted	break
14	Emma	F	39	Canterbury	Cellbank	G3	GCSE or equivalent	yes	10 or under	no	£30,001–£40,000	FT	<10 extra hrs no extra pay	no break, change hours
4	Eric	M	42	Canterbury	Cellbank	G4+	A level or equivalent	yes	11–16	no	£30,001–£40,000	FT	<15 extra hrs no extra pay	no break
125	Estelle	F	54	Sheffield	Shopwell	Shopfloor	No qualifications	yes	17+	yes	£15,001–£20,000	PT	contracted	break
100	Eve	F	47	Sheffield	Council	G6-9	Higher education below degree	yes	10 or under	yes	£15,001–£20,000	PT	flexi, no problems	no break, change hours
120	Faith	F	41	Sheffield	Shopwell	Manager	GCSE or equivalent	yes	11–16	no	£30,001–£40,000	FT	<10 extra hrs no extra pay	break
61	Fiona	F	44	Canterbury	Shopwell	Manager	GCSE or equivalent	yes	17+	no	£30,001–£40,000	FT	<5 extra hrs no extra pay	break
16	Flora	F	41	Canterbury	Cellbank	G4+	A level or equivalent	yes	10 or under	no	£40,001–£50,000	PT	<10 extra hrs no extra pay	no break, change hours
51	Frank	M	48	Canterbury	Shopwell	Shopfloor	GCSE or equivalent	yes	11–16	no	£20,001–£30,000	FT	contracted	no break
33	Fred	M	65	Canterbury	Council	G3	Apprentice	no		no	Less than £15,000	PT	contracted	no break
119	Gemma	F	38	Sheffield	Shopwell	Manager	Degree or equivalent	no		no	£40,001–£50,000	FT	<10 extra hrs no extra pay	no break
53	Gerald	M	61	Canterbury	Shopwell	Shopfloor	No qualifications	yes	17+	no	£15,001–£20,000	FT	extra for overtime	no break

Ref	Pseud-onym	Sex	Age	Location	Sector	Grade	Qualifications	Children	Age of youngest child	Other caring	Annual household income	Contr-acted hours	Actual hours	Career path[a]
118	Gillian	F	38	Sheffield	Shopwell	Shopfloor	GCSE or equivalent	yes	11–16	yes	£20,001–£30,000	PT	extra for overtime	break
19	Glenys	F	49	Canterbury	Cellbank	G1	GCSE or equivalent	yes	17+	yes	£15,001–£20,000	PT	extra for overtime	break
31	Gordon	M	58	Canterbury	Council	G1	Apprentice	yes	17+	no	£20,001–£30,000	PT	extra for overtime	no break
58	Grace	F	41	Canterbury	Shopwell	Manager	GCSE or equivalent	yes	17+	no	£30,001–£40,000	FT	<15 extra hrs no extra pay	no break, change hours
71	Graham	M	44	Sheffield	Cellbank	G6	ACIB	yes	17+	no	£40,001–£50,000	FT	<5 extra hrs no extra pay	no break
74	Greg	M	47	Sheffield	Cellbank	G1	A level or equivalent	no		no	£15,001–£20,000	FT	contracted	no break
76	Hannah	F	27	Sheffield	Cellbank	G3	A level or equivalent	no		no	£40,001–£50,000	FT	contracted	no break
32	Harry	M	62	Canterbury	Council	G1	Apprentice	yes	17+	no	£15,001–£20,000	PT	contracted	no break
63	Helen	F	46	Canterbury	Shopwell	Shopfloor	GCSE or equivalent	yes	17+	no	£30,001–£40,000	PT	extra for overtime	break
84	Holly	F	39	Sheffield	Cellbank	G3	A level or equivalent	yes	10 or under	yes	£40,001–£50,000	PT	contracted	no break, change hours
93	Hugh	M	54	Sheffield	Council	G10+	Degree or equivalent	yes	17+	yes	£30,001–£40,000	FT	occ more no extra pay	no break
45	Ida	F	53	Canterbury	Council	G6-9	A level or equivalent	no		no	£20,001–£30,000	FT	<5 extra hrs no extra pay	no break
122	Ingrid	F	44	Sheffield	Shopwell	Shopfloor	A level or equivalent	yes	17+	yes	Less than £15,000	FT	extra for overtime	break
64	Irene	F	51	Canterbury	Shopwell	Shopfloor	No qualifications	yes	17+	no	Less than £15,000	FT	contracted	break
34	Isobel	F	32	Canterbury	Council	G3	GCSE or equivalent	yes	10 or under	no	£20,001–£30,000	PT	contracted	no break, change hours

Ref	Pseud-onym	Sex	Age	Location	Sector	Grade	Qualifications	Children	Age of youngest child	Other caring	Annual household income	Contr-acted hours	Actual hours	Career path[a]
110	James	M	39	Sheffield	Shopwell	Shopfloor	GCSE or equivalent	yes	10 or under	no	£20,001–£30,000	FT	extra for overtime	no break
38	Janine	F	44	Canterbury	Council	G4-5	A level or equivalent	yes	17+	no	£30,001–£40,000	FT	contracted	break
89	Jason	M	27	Sheffield	Council	G4-5	A level or equivalent	no		no	£15,001–£20,000	FT	contracted	no break
66	Jean	F	58	Canterbury	Shopwell	Shopfloor	No qualifications	yes	17+	no	£15,001–£20,000	PT	extra for overtime	break
11	Jenny	F	37	Canterbury	Cellbank	G2	GCSE or equivalent	yes	10 or under	no	Can't/prefer not to say	PT	extra for overtime	break
109	Jeremy	M	38	Sheffield	Shopwell	Manager	Commercial qualifications	yes	10 or under	no	£30,001–£40,000	FT	<10 extra hrs no extra pay	no break
37	Joyce	F	41	Canterbury	Council	G6-9	Commercial qualifications	yes	10 or under	yes	£30,001–£40,000	FT	<10 extra hrs no extra pay	no break
13	Justine	F	38	Canterbury	Cellbank	G3	GCSE or equivalent	yes	11-16	no	£40,001–£50,000	FT	<5 extra hrs no extra pay	no break, change hours
35	Katie	F	39	Canterbury	Council	G2	GCSE or equivalent	yes	10 or under	no	£20,001–£30,000	FT	contracted	no break, change hours
67	Katrina	F	69	Canterbury	Shopwell	Shopfloor	Apprentice	yes	17+	no	£15,001–£20,000	PT	extra for overtime	break
15	Kerry	F	40	Canterbury	Cellbank	G4+	GCSE or equivalent	yes	10 or under	yes	£30,001–£40,000	FT	<10 extra hrs no extra pay	no break
111	Kevin	M	45	Sheffield	Shopwell	Manager	GCSE or equivalent	yes	11-16	no	More than £50,000	FT	<10 extra hrs no extra pay	no break
62	Laura	F	45	Canterbury	Shopwell	Shopfloor	GCSE or equivalent	no		no	Can't/prefer not to say	FT	contracted	no break
95	Lorna	F	36	Sheffield	Council	G4-5	A level or equivalent	yes	10 or under	yes	£20,001–£30,000	PT	contracted change hours	no break
20	Louise	F	50	Canterbury	Cellbank	G3	A level or equivalent	yes	17+	no	£40,001–£50,000	FT	<5 extra hrs no extra pay	break

Ref	Pseud-onym	Sex	Age	Location	Sector	Grade	Qualifications	Children	Age of youngest child	Other caring	Annual household income	Contr-acted hours	Actual hours	Career path[a]
105	Mabel	F	59	Sheffield	Council	G1	Commercial qualifications	yes	17+	yes	£20,001-£30,000	PT		break
18	Mandy	F	45	Canterbury	Cellbank	G3	GCSE or equivalent	yes	10 or under	no	£40,001-£50,000	PT	extra for overtime	no break, change hours
96	Marcia	F	37	Sheffield	Council	G1	GCSE or equivalent	yes	10 or under	no	£20,001-£30,000	PT	contracted	no break, change hours
97	Marilyn	F	37	Sheffield	Council	G1	A level or equivalent	no		yes	£15,001-£20,000	FT	flexi, no problems	no break
48	Martin	M	36	Canterbury	Shopwell	Manager	GCSE or equivalent	yes	10 or under	no	£40,001-£50,000	FT	<10 extra hrs no extra pay	no break
65	Mary	F	56	Canterbury	Shopwell	Shopfloor	No qualifications	yes	17+	no	Less than £15,000	PT	contracted	break
115	Megan	F	34	Sheffield	Shopwell	Shopfloor	GCSE or equivalent	yes	10 or under	no	Less than £15,000	FT	extra for overtime	break
92	Mervyn	M	51	Sheffield	Council	G10+	Postgrad qualification	yes	17+	yes	£30,001-£40,000	FT	contracted	no break
7	Mike	M	45	Canterbury	Cellbank	G3	A level or equivalent	yes	10 or under	no	£20,001-£30,000	FT	<10 extra hrs no extra pay	no break
41	Miriam	F	49	Canterbury	Council	G3	SEN	yes	17+	yes	£15,001-£20,000	FT	contracted	break
44	Molly	F	52	Canterbury	Council	G3	Commercial qualifications	yes	17+	yes	£20,001-£30,000	FT	contracted	break
102	Nadine	F	48	Sheffield	Council	G10+	Higher education below degree	yes	17+	no	More than £50,000	FT	<5 extra hrs no extra pay	break
104	Nancy	F	57	Sheffield	Council	G1	GCSE or equivalent	yes	17+	no	£15,001-£20,000	FT	contracted	break
101	Naomi	F	47	Sheffield	Council	G10+	Degree or equivalent	yes	10 or under	no	More than £50,000	FT	occ more no extra pay	no break, change hours
75	Natalie	F	21	Sheffield	Cellbank	G1	A level or equivalent	no		no	£20,001-£30,000	FT	contracted	no break
69	Neil	M	31	Sheffield	Cellbank	G2	GCSE or equivalent	no		no	£20,001-£30,000	FT	contracted	no break

Ref	Pseud-onym	Sex	Age	Location	Sector	Grade	Qualifications	Children	Age of youngest child	Other caring	Annual household income	Contr-acted hours	Actual hours	Career path[a]
21	Nerys	F	53	Canterbury	Cellbank	G1	GCSE or equivalent	yes	17+	no	£40,001–£50,000	PT	contracted	break
8	Norman	M	47	Canterbury	Cellbank	G3	A level or equivalent	yes	10 or under	no	£20,001–£30,000	FT	<5 extra hrs no extra pay	no break
36	Olga	F	41	Canterbury	Council	G6–9	Degree or equivalent	yes	10 or under	no	£40,001–£50,000	PT	contracted	no break, change hours
72	Oliver	M	44	Sheffield	Cellbank	G4+	ACIB	yes	10 or under	no	More than £50,000	FT	many extra hrs no extra pay	no break
40	Olivia	F	48	Canterbury	Council	G1	GCSE or equivalent	yes	11–16	no	£30,001–£40,000	PT	contracted	break
42	Patsy	F	51	Canterbury	Council	G10+	Degree or equivalent	yes	17+	no	Can't/prefer not to say	FT	<10 extra hrs no extra pay	break
80	Pauline	F	35	Sheffield	Cellbank	G4+	GCSE or equivalent	no		no	£30,001–£40,000	FT	<10 extra hrs no extra pay	no break
25	Pearl	F	59	Canterbury	Cellbank	G1	GCSE or equivalent	yes	17+	yes	£30,001–£40,000	FT	<5 extra hrs no extra pay	break
85	Peggy	F	45	Sheffield	Cellbank	G4+	Degree or equivalent	yes	11–16	no	More than £50,000	FT	<10 extra hrs no extra pay	break
5	Philip	M	42	Canterbury	Cellbank	G3	A level or equivalent	yes	10 or under	yes	£30,001–£40,000	FT	<5 extra hrs no extra pay	no break
81	Poppy	F	37	Sheffield	Cellbank	G3	GCSE or equivalent	no	10 or under	no	£40,001–£50,000	FT	<10 extra hrs no extra pay	no break
24	Rachel	F	59	Canterbury	Cellbank	G2	GCSE or equivalent	yes	17+	yes	Can't/prefer not to say	PT	contracted	break
91	Richard	M	39	Sheffield	Council	G3	Degree or equivalent	yes	10 or under	no	£30,001–£40,000	FT	contracted	no break
98	Rita	F	40	Sheffield	Council	G4–5	Postgrad qualification	yes	10 or under	no	£30,001–£40,000	PT	flexi, no problems	no break, change hours
68	Robin	M	26	Sheffield	Cellbank	G4+	A level or equivalent	no		no	£20,001–£30,000	FT	<5 extra hrs no extra pay	no break

Ref	Pseudonym	Sex	Age	Location	Sector	Grade	Qualifications	Children	Age of youngest child	Other caring	Annual household income	Contracted hours	Actual hours	Career path[a]
43	Rosa	F	51	Canterbury	Council	G1	Commercial qualifications	yes	17+	no	£20,001–£30,000	PT	extra for overtime	break
73	Rupert	M	46	Sheffield	Cellbank	G4+	ACIB	yes	17+	no	£30,001–£40,000	FT	<10 extra hrs no extra pay	no break
46	Sandy	F	58	Canterbury	Council	G1	GCSE or equivalent	yes	17+	no	£20,001–£30,000	FT	contracted	break
3	Scott	M	34	Canterbury	Cellbank	G3	GCSE or equivalent	yes	10 or under	no	£30,001–£40,000	FT	<5 extra hrs no extra pay	no break
107	Sean	M	30	Sheffield	Shopwell	Shopfloor	Apprentice	yes	10 or under	no	Less than £15,000	FT	extra for overtime	no break
94	Shauna	F	34	Sheffield	Council	G6-9	A level or equivalent	yes	10 or under	no	More than £50,000	PT	contracted	no break, change hours
10	Sheila	F	34	Canterbury	Cellbank	G2	Commercial qualifications	yes	10 or under	no	£30,001–£40,000	FT	contracted	no break, change hours
87	Shirley	F	47	Sheffield	Cellbank	G3	GCSE or equivalent	no		no	£20,001–£30,000	FT	extra for overtime	no break
79	Sigrid	F	33	Sheffield	Cellbank	G2	A level or equivalent	yes	10 or under	no	£15,001–£20,000	PT	contracted change hours	no break
47	Simon	M	26	Canterbury	Shopwell	Shopfloor	GCSE or equivalent	no		no	Can't/prefer not to say	FT	contracted	no break
116	Sophie	F	35	Sheffield	Shopwell	Shopfloor	GCSE or equivalent	yes	10 or under	yes	Less than £15,000	PT	extra for overtime	break
121	Sylvia	F	43	Sheffield	Shopwell	Shopfloor	GCSE or equivalent	yes	17+	no	£30,001–£40,000	FT	<10 extra hrs no extra pay	no break, change hours
26	Terry	M	28	Canterbury	Council	G4-5	Postgrad qualification	no		no	£20,001–£30,000	FT	<15 extra hrs no extra pay	no break
88	Tessa	F	49	Sheffield	Cellbank	G1	GCSE or equivalent	yes	11-16	yes	£20,001–£30,000	PT	extra for overtime	break

Ref	Pseud-onym	Sex	Age	Location	Sector	Grade	Qualifications	Children	Age of youngest child	Other caring	Annual household income	Contr-acted hours	Actual hours	Career path[a]
123	Thea	F	48	Sheffield	Shopwell	Shopfloor	GCSE or equivalent	yes	17+	yes	£20,001–£30,000	PT	<5 extra hrs no extra pay	break
82	Trudy	F	37	Sheffield	Cellbank	G3	GCSE or equivalent	yes	10 or under	no	£20,001–£30,000	FT	contracted	no break, change hours
39	Ursula	F	44	Canterbury	Council	G10+	Degree or equivalent	yes	10 or under	no	More than £50,000	FT	<10 extra hrs no extra pay	no break
17	Vicky	F	42	Canterbury	Cellbank	G4+	GCSE or equivalent	no		yes	£40,001–£50,000	FT	<10 extra hrs no extra pay	no break
77	Zoe	F	29	Sheffield	Cellbank	G4+	GCSE or equivalent	yes	10 or under	no	More than £50,000	FT	<5 extra hrs no extra pay	no break

Note: [a] Break includes actually leaving a job or reducing hours from full-time to part-time. It does not include statutory maternity leave.

Also available from The Policy Press
Published in association with the Joseph Rowntree Foundation

Family and Work series: selected titles

Family and work in minority ethnic businesses

Anuradha Basu and Eser Altinay

While the Labour government has initiated policies to address growing concerns regarding the spillover effects of work on family life, little is known about the effects on family life of self-employment among minority ethnic groups, despite the higher incidence of self-employment among them. This report redresses this neglect by examining work–life balance issues in family-run minority ethnic businesses.

Paperback £13.95 ISBN 1 86134 548 8
297 x 210mm 52 pages November 2003

Caring and counting
The impact of mothers' employment on family relationships

Tracey Reynolds, Claire Callender and Rosalind Edwards

The main work–life balance policies promoted by government focus on the amount of time mothers spend at work. This report challenges this approach. It suggests that what happens inside the workplace and how this interacts with family life is just as important.

Paperback £14.95 ISBN 1 86134 534 8
297 x 210mm 76 pages July 2003

Combining self-employment and family life

Alice Bell and Ivana La Valle

Despite the increasing policy interest in work–life balance issues, relatively little research has been carried out into the links between self-employment and family life. This report considers, for the first time, the extent to which new family-friendly initiatives and legislation provide adequate support for self-employed parents.

Paperback £13.95 ISBN 1 86134 533 X
297 x 210mm 64 pages June 2003

Around the clock
Childcare services at atypical times

June Statham and Ann Mooney

This timely report considers how childcare services are meeting the needs of parents working atypical hours.

Paperback £11.95 ISBN 1 86134 502 X
297 x 210mm 44 pages June 2003

Geographical mobility
Family impacts

Anne E. Green and Angela Canny

This report charts the changing role and nature of geographical mobility in organisational strategies and career development. It explores the work and family life experiences of employees and partners who have faced job-related geographical mobility.

Paperback £13.95 ISBN 1 86134 466 X
297 x 210mm 68 pages May 2003

Running around in circles
Coordinating childcare, education and work

Christine Skinner

Drawing on detailed interviews with mothers, this study explores how parents manage to coordinate the childcare and educational needs of all children in the family with their working arrangements. Uniquely, it adopts a family unit perspective to consider how these needs are managed.

Paperback £13.95 ISBN 1 86134 501 1
297 x 210mm 64 pages May 2003

For further information about the Family and Work series and other titles published by The Policy Press, please visit our website at: **www.policypress.org.uk** or telephone +44 (0)117 331 4054

To order, please contact:
Marston Book Services • PO Box 269
Abingdon• Oxon OX14 4YN, UK
Tel: +44 (0)1235 465500
Fax: +44 (0)1235 465556
E-mail: direct.orders@marston.co.uk